IF SHE HAD A CHOICE, WOULD SHE BUY FROM YOU?

"Go ahead: imagine yourself as the top salesperson at your company. Continue on to see most of your leads coming to you as referrals. Even more, imagine your customers spreading the word about how terrific you are to everyone they know. Now, let's take it even further: Imagine the largest consumer market—women—singing your praises and making you rich."   —*From the Preface*

To many sales professionals, understanding women customers is a daily challenge: the way women interpret behavior, hear unexpected meanings, take in "peripheral" information, and how they view the overall sales process. As a result, women's wants, needs, and expectations are often misunderstood.

Winning the Toughest Customer reveals how readers can maneuver this complex market segment by providing the tools to customize selling to women, and then to anybody else. This notable guide shows professionals how to meet the expectations of female customers and benefit from women's legendary loyalty and viral marketing potential.

Readers will learn about:

- Gender differences and strategy
- Effective communication techniques
- Relationship-building
- Strategic positioning
- Maneuvering the road to close
- The added value of brand-loyal women

Author and industry expert **Delia Passi** shatters gender and sales myths with boldness and humor, enabling salespeople and entrepreneurs to properly communicate and close the deal with the most influential buying market segment in the world.

Internationally recognized sales and marketing expert **Delia Passi** is President and CEO of Medelia, Inc., a leading marketing and consulting agency that helps companies gain market share of women consumers. Passi is also the Founder of WomenCertified®, the Seal of Approval that women trust and recognize, to show case your business as WomenFriendly®. Passi has trained thousands of sales associates to sell more effectively to women through her own series of sales training programs, and she has developed highly successful communication strategies for Fortune 500 companies such as Wachovia Bank, Principal Financial, Merrill Lynch, Harley-Davidson, Wells Fargo, Trek, TD Ameritrade and more... She is the former Vice President of the Working Woman Network and Group Publisher of *Working Woman* and *Working Mother* magazines.

Call Delia Passi today for a special offer from WomenCertified to help build your business among women!

Toll free: (866) 937-6996

"WomenCertified is creating a customer service revolution for women by setting the standard of excellence in customer service."

      –Delia Passi, Founder

Awarded the WomenCertified Seal® for excellence in communicating to women. A registered trademark of Medelia, Inc.

WINNING THE
TOUGHEST
CUSTOMER

DELIA PASSI
WITH A. B. ARONSON

WINNING THE TOUGHEST CUSTOMER

(THE ESSENTIAL GUIDE TO SELLING TO WOMEN)

KAPLAN) PUBLISHING

President and Publisher: Maureen McMahon
Acquisitions Editor: Karen Murphy
Development Editor: Trey Thoelcke
Production Editor: Leah Strauss
Interior Design: Lucy Jenkins
Cover Design: Michael Warrell
Typesetter: Todd Bowman

© 2006 by Delia Passi

Published by Kaplan Publishing, a division of Kaplan, Inc.

Printed in the United States of America

ISBN-10: 1-60714-523-5   ISBN-13: 978-1-60714-523-3

Kaplan Publishing books are available at special quantity discounts to use for sales promotions, employee premiums, or educational purposes. Please call our Special Sales Department to order or for more information at 212-618-2414, e-mail kevin.cooper@kaplan.com, or write to Kaplan Publishing, 1 Liberty Plaza, 24th Floor, New York, NY 10006.

This book is dedicated to those
who respect the equality of the sexes
but appreciate their differences and
reflect that in their actions.

(contents)

(preface)

Can you imagine what it would be like to find a hidden treasure or win the lottery? To suddenly have lots more money to live the way you've always dreamed? Well, winning that game is a one-in-a-million chance and unlikely to happen to you or anyone you know. But there is a way to actively pursue that kind of money. It will take some effort, some understanding, some change—but not as much as you might think—to bring a lottery-level payoff within your grasp.

Go ahead: Imagine yourself as the top salesperson at your company. Continue to see most of your leads coming to you as referrals. Even more, imagine your customers spreading the word about how terrific you are to everyone they know. Now, let's take it even further: Imagine the largest consumer market—women—singing your praises and making you rich.

Hello, and welcome to a salesperson's dream, where millions of eager customers are seeking that one-in-a-million salesperson who truly "gets it"—and that salesperson is you. That's what this book is about. Getting into the biggest game around—and learning what it takes to win. Beginning right now, let's stop imagining what *could* be and get to work. From here on, we'll focus on what we can do to make it what *will* be.

If you want it, you can get it—but you need to strike one bargain first. Accept that women are the toughest customers out there, but that getting their business is worth the work. A recent research study of 10,000 consumers recently reported that, *"When it comes to brands, a woman expects different things than a man. The brand she uses must not only perform the way she wants it to, it must treat her the way she wants to be treated, on her own terms, to give her a sense of community and make her feel as if she's part of something special."* That's the kind of field you'll be playing on.

I've heard people call it everything from the hormonal flip to conversing in an alien language. The differences may be less complicated than that, but they are real. At the outset you need to know that women follow more elaborate processes to decide and buy. They tend to expect more service and more nuanced communication than other customers might. If you are open-minded enough to accept that selling to men and selling to women is different, and that's OK, then you've got what it takes to get into a trillion-dollar market—and stay there, sustained by referrals and positive word of mouth—for keeps.

In numerous traditionally male-dominated industries, such as financial services, auto, and home improvement, the potential of the women's market is virtually untapped. What's more, as you will learn, when you meet the needs of a woman, you will exceed the expectations of a man. That means this book can equip you with the tools you need to sell almost anything better to almost anyone! Now that's the way to get ahead.

So what makes me a nationally recognized authority on selling to women? It's a culmination of amazing sales and training experiences. Fresh out of college in 1981, I began my career selling copiers for Xerox, mostly to male business owners. At that time, there were only a small percentage of business owners who were women, and I hadn't encountered

many. Xerox was and still is known for its great training, but nothing prepared me for what I encountered.
In short, I saw that women are the toughest customers, but, when treated right in the sales process, they
can become the best customers. This insight informed
a major evolution in my sales process—and success.

In the early 1990s I entered the world of publishing, and by 1998 I was publisher of *Working
Mother* magazine. During that transition, I suddenly
had to sell more to women than to men; more than
70 percent of our customer base comprised women
decision makers. I found that by modifying my
sales approach to accommodate a woman's buying
style, I could increase my close rate significantly.
When I became publisher, I immediately trained
my sales force on the techniques for selling to
women that I had developed for myself. Our first
year, our sales volume was up by 36 percent, and
by the second, we continued to exceed sales by 42
percent.

In 2001, I chose to start MedeliaCommunications,
which quickly became the leading marketing and
sales training company specializing in women consumers. I love to train men and women on how best

to market and sell to women; it's a passion, and also the most satisfying job I have ever had, because I know that my training has transformed careers and businesses.

With this book, I hope to transform yours.

(acknowledgments)

Selling is my passion. For that I thank my dad, who I consider one of the best salesmen I know. Without knowing it, he taught me to value a customer above all, and to sell to them the way they want to be sold to. I also get enormous gratification from helping others succeed. For that I thank my mom, who finds ways to help and care for others each day. You are both so precious and have been such a driving force in my life.

This book is a dream realized, and without my writing partner, Amy Aronson, this would not have been possible. She is one of the most extraordinary women I know, with degrees to intimidate most of us and the patience of a saint to manage a CEO who was preoccupied with running an extraordinarily fast growing company.

As I believe success is attributed to those who surround you, I give a special thanks to my team at

MedeliaCommunications for their commitment to our growth and mission—to be a true partner to our clients. And a special word of appreciation to my publishing team at Kaplan for their confidence and commitment to the success of this book.

From my heart I thank the people in my life that have made each day a blessing. To my daughters, Diana, Stefanie, Jaclyn, and my stepdaughter Emily— you are my constant source of inspiration and pride. And to my husband Greg, who is my partner in all I do, my sounding board, my business advisor, my emotional support, and my insight into the inner workings of the male mind. Thank you mostly for giving me wings to fly.

A final thank you to you. Without your desire to learn and grow, this book would be irrelevant.

(introduction)

Why Play To Win
the Toughest Customer?

When I do sales training around the country, the most common question I hear concerns why women take so much longer than men to close the sale. In fact, my original title for this book was *Why Does She Take So Long?*

The second most common questions are more universal expressions of that concern with differences: Why doesn't a woman customer act more like a man? Where is she coming from? What does she expect from me?

Over the years, I've heard these same questions so many times that now I start my presentations by asking them myself. I do it with humor—which, by the way, women tend to love.

There's an old joke that goes something like this:

A man is walking on the beach in California when God speaks to him from the heavens. God says, "You've been a good, hardworking man all your life, so I'm going to grant you one wish." The man quickly replies, "I have always dreamed of traveling to Hawaii, of reaching a paradise like that—so filled with lush rewards.

"But," adds the man, "there's one problem. I don't like to fly. I would like to drive from here to Hawaii. Would you build me a bridge to Hawaii?"

To that, the Almighty responds, "Even for God that's a monumental task. All the architecture, design, and building of a thing like that . . . The concrete and structure that must extend for miles and miles across the vast Pacific . . . Isn't there anything else I can grant you?"

The man considers for a minute. "Well, I've always wanted to have better relationships with women. Can you please help me to better understand women?"

"OK," God quickly replies, "so how many lanes do you want on that bridge?"

OK, so maybe God is not that challenged by women, but we mortal men and women all struggle at times to find a clear understanding of how to communicate with or, in this case, sell to women. Even men at the top of their game say women pose a serious challenge to winning in the marketplace. The way women interpret your behavior, your words; the way they respond to your solutions; what they notice; what they want; and maybe most of all, *what they expect* often seems to make no sense. Questions seem to come from left field. What was she talking about? What gives?

Many men tell me that a woman customer seems like another country—and they feel like foreign travelers, trying to make their way without a map. Men like to "just do it." It's about direction and action: Let's get to the point, solve the problem, close the sale, and move on. If there's any other talk, that's part of the game—and both of the men involved know how and why to play.

But women can seem like documented aliens, outliers, wildcards. They just aren't with the same program. What's with "just browsing"?—what makes them primed to buy? Why don't they just make a decision instead of talking with everyone they know? I get the problem—why won't they just buy my solution? What do they want from me? Lost for common ground, many salespeople get frustrated; some even get fed up. They interrupt women, dominate the conversation, think they can "mind read" women's needs—or bag it and walk away. Any of these moves may feel right at the time, but each is a very bad call—180 degrees wrong. They are some of the surest bets for losing a woman's business, probably forever.

Everybody knows that women are the tougher sex to sell to. There are rules to the game and they just don't seem to get them. Well, here's the little secret at the heart of this book that readers can take to the bank: *Women* are *different kinds of customers than men. They* do *operate under a different set of rules. But there is method to the madness. And there's a big payoff in knowing what it is.* If you understand where she's coming from, you'll have a powerful selling tool to mine the largest major market on planet Earth. What's more, the sky is the limit. Once you know how to sell to women, you can sell better to anyone. All you need is the playbook. And this is it.

Learning to sell well to women means selling well to the toughest customers. It means starting with the hardest nut to crack. *Research shows that when you meet the expectations of women, you exceed the expectations of men*—so that's a no-brainer. But the lightbulb is this: Once you can deliver what women want in the purchasing process, you'll have the tools to win with all kinds of new customers. With the techniques in this book, you may be able to increase your sales and overall business effectiveness with any and every client.

Years ago, we had transactional selling. Then came relationship selling. You're due for the next level: target selling—which means selling to anyone and everyone the way they want to be sold to, the way that will make them want to buy from you and keep them coming back to you for more.

Anyone trying to get ahead in today's changing economy must listen up or lose out. The business world and the marketplace will never again be segregated or divided into men's and women's "separate spheres." Today, a whole spectrum of new customers shares the world—at work and at play, at home and on the road, in business and in pleasure. Everything now depends on figuring out the connection, on "getting" where the other is coming from. Anything less means having less of whatever the relationship has to offer.

And they have a lot to offer salespeople. More than 60 percent of high-net-worth women have earned their own fortunes. Three quarters (75 percent) of women executives in the Fortune 500 outearn their husbands. The women's market today is approaching $4 trillion. That's close to the gross domestic product of Japan ($4.8 trillion). If you pocketed the annual team payrolls of the top pro sports—that's the NFL ($2.14 billion), NBA ($1.55 billion), MLB ($2.15 billion), and the NHL, when last it operated ($1.4 billion)—it would take 500 years to amass as much money as women control right now.

A key word here is "control." *Even if the woman doesn't make the money in the household, she's the one who* spends *it*. Women make or influence over 80 percent of all purchases made in America today. Even among those who work full-time, the vast majority, or 72 percent, are still the primary shoppers for themselves, their homes, and their families.

See for yourself. Just go to the mall. Who is there, and spending more money than any other market segment?

Look no farther than your own front door. Or talk to your buddies. Who is it that controls family finances? Who ultimately picks the car, the kids' computers, the TVs, CDs, and furniture? Who buys the food, the clothing, the shoes, the gifts, the family's entertainment? Who ultimately decides about the insurance, the health care plan, the real estate agent, the credit cards, the home equity loan? When was the last time you made all the travel arrangements for your family vacation?

If you think her influence is strong now, that's just a taste of things to come.

Item: Women have outnumbered men on college campuses since 1979, and in graduate schools since 1984.

Item: Women are 50 percent of the students in the high-earning professions of law and medicine; 35 percent of those earning MBAs.

Item: Right now, there are more than 3 million women earning managerial salaries in the private sector alone.

Did You Know?

Women purchase 83 percent of all products and services including

- 80 percent of all health care;
- 55 percent of bank choice;
- 50 percent of all business travel;
- 65 percent of herbal remedies, vitamins, and minerals;
- 66 percent of all autos (and influence 85 percent of purchases);
- 50 percent of all computers; and
- 90 percent of all jewelry, perfume, and related items.

Item: Women entrepreneurs are starting businesses at more than twice the rate of men, and those with revenues of more than $10 million have grown by about 40 percent since 1997.

Item: A massive transfer of wealth is about to begin. In the next ten years—by 2015—at least $15 trillion will land in the hands of baby boomer women. More than $40 trillion is expected to pass from one generation to the next by 2044, much of it through or to the hands of women. (Face it, at some time in their lives, nearly all women—more than 90 percent—have sole charge of the family's assets.)

Clearly, when you have something, anything, to sell, she is the one to speak to—but you've got to know how to do it.

This book will tell you how. It is your playbook to a new playing field that, if you know how to navigate it, is ripe with rewards. Take in just a chapter a day, and in about a week you'll be ready to go after the business of your dreams. Or take it on a plane ride as travel reading. Or read it in an evening. In nine brief, clear, realistic, and solution-oriented chapters, you will learn the step-by-step essentials to customize your selling first to women, and then perhaps to anybody else. You will learn simple specifics about how to talk, how to listen, how to evolve the process, how to pace the interaction, how to present yourself, how to provide the right kind of service—in other words, how to create the connection you need to get business done, and maintain a relationship that over time will redouble your success.

Research shows that female customers are uncommonly loyal to products and services that prove themselves worthy. Some 86 percent of women business owners will buy the same products and services for home as they do for the office. You do the math:

If you can sell a woman once, you may already have sold to her again and again and again.

And women talk—especially to one another. This makes them natural viral marketers. Good word of mouth from women consumers can mean exponential growth in new business. All you have to do is know how to become the one-in-a-million sales professional she trusts.

Bottom line: If you want to be in it to win, this market is where you've got to be good. Women's lives have changed dramatically in a relatively short time, and every bit of evidence says they will keep going forward—right in sync with the diversifying American marketplace. This book will teach you to speak the customer's language—any customer's language—whatever its origin, inflection, orientation, or direction. By knowing how to deal with differences in communication and buying styles, you will negotiate and sell well to any kind of client. And it might not hurt your personal life either.

Beginning with the immense women's market, this easy-to-follow book can enable you to navigate the new American marketplace, taking you any place you have ever wanted to go.

chapter one

The New Playing Field

Today's Women's Market

Salesperson Rick escorts prospective customer Sandra to the door and shakes her hand, then turns back to his office.

Rick (to himself): "That went great. I managed to hit every selling point and ask all the important questions. I'm sure she's confident that we're the ones to do business with. She'll go home, get permission from her husband, and probably bring him back and sign the papers. If I don't hear from her by the end of the week, I'll follow up."

Sandra (to herself): "What a waste of time, and like I have time to waste! I don't think he listened once to what I was saying, or maybe he was too preoccupied trying to get through his pitch. I hope I find someone soon who will be the right person to handle my business. This is so frustrating."

Selling is a communication process. Communication means the transmission of ideas or information. With women, the communication process becomes a bit more complex than just making your pitch or gathering information. It's apparent through my many years of training salespeople that selling to women is harder than selling to men. Women take longer, need more input, expect more attentive service, require more follow-up, and more. I've heard the same story over and over: Women are far tougher customers to do business with, and they demand more service than men.

So why bother? By now you already know the drill. For one thing, anyone who succeeds in selling and servicing women customers will tell you that the extra effort will pay you back in multiples. You could say that $1 + 1 = 3$. That means, sell well to one woman and she will reward you with her business, her loyalty (more business), and probably a large number of referrals to other women (and the beat goes on).

For another, there's an even larger payoff as well: Once you can effectively sell, market to, and retain women customers, you'll have the tools to sell anything better to anyone. Men may not need the extra attention—but they will appreciate it. And almost any target market you can name demands attentive adjustments to their way of shopping, deciding, and buying. Think minority markets. Think ethnic markets. Think baby boomers. Think seniors. Think about it: That means a lot of new business.

Women are the prime consumers in our country. It's women who buy most of everything sold. But the new context, the playing field, is this: We're not talking only clothes and groceries anymore. The women's market has expanded in every direction— and is on track to keep going. Women today purchase it all, even what not that long ago was strictly guy stuff, such as cars, computers, real estate, and stocks. Think about this: Women now buy the majority of all new cars sold in America. They buy more electronic gizmos than men do. And they don't need anyone's permission any more.

Now whether she likes the sales experience or not, eventually she's got to buy from someone. But when given a choice, a woman will go out of her way to do business with someone who provides the experience she prefers.

True story: A good friend, who also happens to be a successful woman business owner in need of a new car, went shopping at a variety of dealers and was turned off by the experience she had at all but one. That dealer provided an excellent experience, treated her with respect as the decision maker, and forged a relationship with her that resulted in her buying their brand. Unfortunately for her, though, she is not all that pleased with the car and it was not her first choice, but she was so impressed by the salesman and found the encounter so favorable that she chose the relationship over the product. (Her regret is that she didn't find the right product along with the right relationship, but that's another story.)

What does this mean to you? *As a salesperson, you can create an advantage for your product by providing an experience that can't be found with your competitors.*

Being the first one on your block to master the technique of selling to women is also more valuable than her business alone. Let's face it: Women talk. They like to share stories and compare notes. They care about sparing their friends or family unpleasant experiences. A recent personal experience tells it like it is. I was walking into an auto dealership to check out a new vehicle. As I approached the door, a woman was exiting and told me, "I wouldn't go in there alone if I were you. I was standing around waiting the longest time for someone to help me. It's as though they couldn't care less about my business. Probably because I'm a woman buying a car on my own." And she marched out the door. I thanked her, and entered, hesitant already, and disinclined to buy from that dealer.

That woman was unlikely to stop at sharing her bad experience just with me, a stranger. I'd bet on at least a handful of conversations with other women before she gets it out of her system. Nobody likes feeling disregarded. But women also live by communication more than men do, and they use communication almost instinctually, it seems, to caretake and to protect others.

Maybe it is instinct—or, at least, biology. Women ponder their experiences—sometimes too much. Biological studies have revealed that when women get upset, their hormone level stays raised for up to 24 hours. Think about that; even a whole day after a bad experience, a woman may still be turning over in her mind what happened. Men tend to brush off issues much faster than women and not chew on them over time, but a woman may experience her bad experience over and over—and talk about it time and again as a means of understanding it, healing, and moving on.

Whatever may be the reason, that woman's negative referrals will slow traffic into that dealership just like they would any other business. Now here's the flipside: A similar positive referral would do just the opposite. A positive impression, the biological theory goes, would linger with a woman longer as well. And a woman's positive word of mouth would achieve higher volume than a man's would, too. Now hear this: Women are twice as likely as men to make referrals. A recent financial survey found that women will make referrals 28 times in regard to a trusted advisor versus only 13 times for men.

There is no getting around the fact of women's talk and their tendency to work it in particular ways. What do they find to talk about so much? The Census Bureau reports that every day women spend about 30 percent more time than men do shopping for goods and services. So, it might just be what kind of shopping or sales experience she just had. And if it made an impression on her, it will probably make an impression on the people she tells about it. And then the people *they* tell about it. And on, and on, like a virus, her word of mouth continues to spread, both the good and bad.

A recent brand study of 10,000 consumers uncovered this compelling finding:

"When it comes to brands, women expect different things than men. The brand she uses must not only perform the way she wants it to, it must treat her the way she wants to be treated on her own terms, to give her a sense of community and make her feel as if she's part of something special."

Wunderman Brand Study

The New Woman Customer

Make no mistake, women today control trillions of dollars, and that's only going to grow. Women have the discretionary and disposable income to buy much more of whatever they want. And they have the authority to buy in many more areas, or, as I like to think, with "many different hats on." Female consumers are buying for households, for family, for their businesses, for corporations, for partners, for themselves as women, for leisure, for investment, for fun . . . They are the largest and best growth market out there—and they are never going back again.

Just look at the numbers: Women are continuing to make huge strides in their public and professional lives. For the first time, in 2004 more women than men were admitted to Harvard's freshman class. Women are now half (49.7 percent) of all medical students, half (49.4 percent) of all law students, and 35 percent of all students enrolled in MBA programs. Across the board, women are getting the degrees that drive success forever after. By 2012, women are projected to hold more than 56 percent of *all* advanced degrees in the United States.

These well-educated women are the ones who will go on to become the high earners in the professions—and in corporate America. According to Catalyst, currently women hold the majority—50.5 percent—of management and professional jobs, even though they make up only 46.5 percent of the U.S. labor force.

A good number of these high-level women will go on to start their own businesses, opening up a whole new area for their purchasing power—and preferences. Already the Census Bureau reports that *nearly half* (47.5 percent) of all privately held businesses in the United States are majority woman-owned.

Impressive as the start-up stats are, the even bigger story is growth. Women-owned firms are growing large—and profitable. Since 1997

- employment has grown at twice the rate of all firms;
- sales growth is ahead of all firms; and
- firms with revenues of more than $10 million have grown by about 40 percent;

All that spells serious money to spend.

And here's another rich statistic for you: Women are more likely than men to start businesses with revenues of more than $1 million, according to the Center for Women's Business Research. That is, women are more likely than men to *start* these successful businesses for themselves—rather than to inherit, purchase, or acquire them in some other way. That means more and more women are seasoned big buyers, and their track record suggests they'll be buying even more and better as time goes on.

Alongside their growing stature as consumers are women's ever-greater self-awareness, self-confidence, and savvy in the marketplace. Today, women are out there, both on their own and right next to men in the workplace, on the highways, and in every leisure activity. They are making their own decisions about how to build a career, how to live, why to invest, what to drive, what to wear, where to travel, and when and whether to own a home. At the same time, female consumers are still largely running American households—and these little organizational units have become more complex and product-driven than ever before.

Now that their lives have grown, women act even more decisively not only as buyers, but also as gatekeepers and deal breakers. *Clearly, we are well past*

*the era of the dependent woman, whose access to
financial wherewithal and purchasing decision making was more passive and secondhand. The new breed
of woman consumer today is educated, informed,
and more empowered than ever.* She has probably
learned something about how to play the game the
old way, but now has the awareness to resent it when
it doesn't fit her style or meet her needs.

The Woman Consumer?

Hold the phone: The idea of "women's way of
buying" seems a little too simple. All women are not
alike. Career women aren't the same as homemakers,
are they? Older women don't come from the same
world as younger women do. And what about diversity? Everywhere today we're hearing that to capture
diversity markets you've got to target your messag-
ing, to speak to consumers in their own language
and where they live.

True enough. There are differences among
women—some of them major. You're right if you're
thinking that not all roads can lead to Rome.

When it comes to women, though, you can't just add color and stir. You've got to adapt your marketing, selling, and negotiating to suit differing values, priorities and preferences that are big parts of what a different culture is. You've got to adapt your entire approach, not just dress it up in pink.

Case in point: As the former publisher of *Working Woman* magazine, I was asked by a financial services client for help. They were disappointed that they'd had little return on investment from a significant advertising campaign targeting women. To better help our client understand what went wrong, we surveyed 2,000 women—and found the results surprising. Actually, that experience planted the seed for this book. The women responded clearly that the marketing message must correspond with the sales experience. While the financial firm wanted to attract more female investors, the company failed to equip its sales force with the tools and insight needed to fulfill the marketing message and become the brand of choice among women. In short, they tried to just add pink and stir—and that is not enough.

A costly lesson learned:

Marketing can drive awareness and interest. Marketing can modify behavior and change perceptions. Marketing can build buzz. But that's where the buck stops. What ultimately drives purchase is the sales and customer experience. That means marketing will not have the sales impact without the sales or user experience matching the marketing promise.

There's also this: Although we recognize a one-size-does-not-fit-all approach, I have found that women from a wide variety of backgrounds still tend to share some gender characteristics as communicators and customers. Women business owners of color often show purchasing styles more similar to other women business owners than to male entrepreneurs, even those of similar background. I've seen moms of many backgrounds share styles more similar to one another than to dads from the same group. Research as well as experience shows that businesswomen buying for work want much the same process as wives buying for their households: Both tend to emphasize research and relationships;

both will probably want more service and follow-up than men do.

Bottom line: There are definite differences among women, but there is also plenty of common ground. Major similarities link their buying styles—and these can help you make your way. Women Baby Boomers, women of a certain age, women executives, you name it—you can probably start the selling process by understanding their common tendencies as women. It's legit to talk and sell to a "women's market" because for all the dizzying differences you can name, there are some large commonalities that can give you a foothold with a wide spectrum of women customers.

And I cannot say often enough that that foothold could be worth a fortune. Here's one knockout gender tendency: Women often cross over in their purchasing preferences—from business to household use, and from themselves to their families. Whether they are wearing their "lawyer" hat or "mom" hat or "homeowner" hat or "me" hat, they are more likely than men to trust the same products, services, and purchasing experience. Some 86 percent of all women business owners say they use the same products in their homes as they do in the office—provided, of course, they are happy with product performance and sales support.

That alone means that if you sell correctly to a woman—any woman—once, you may already have a jump on her future business. And to a large extent, you may have already sold to her again and again elsewhere in her life.

And don't forget her loyalty over time. If she feels she's been listened to, understood, and treated right, you're looking at her repeat business for years as her children, her home, her business, her life, grow. As far as that goes, get this: Almost two thirds of women between 35 and 74 say that disposable income increases as they age—and that they will use their

---

Did you know?

- Women recognize, by a 3:1 ratio, companies that market to women.
- By a 7:1 ratio, women will go out of their way to do business with those companies.

A study by *Working Woman*

money to upgrade the products and services in their lives. That suggests just how lucrative her loyalty can be long term.

Making Your Way to Customization

The other aspect of playing to win in the women's market is this: It is a real route to customization. Once you master some essential skills for selling better to women, you'll have captured the mindset and the tools you need to begin targeting your sales approach to all kinds of markets. At that outset you will have committed yourself to accepting customer differences. That alone will start you on the right path to negotiating and selling better to those women who are exceptions to the rule—and to almost any other individual customer or client.

Think about it: to sell well to a woman, you'll need an expanded skill set. You'll need to know how to speak her language, how to listen and *hear* her, how to create her idea of a comfortable sales experience, how to be patient and respectful, how to establish a relationship of trust that will last, and more. You'll need to develop better relationship skills, better networking skills, attentive service. That kind of in-tune attention can give you an advantage with any customer. It might be especially valued by women and diversity consumers, who haven't enjoyed that kind of respect in the past. But the truth is I've never met a customer who wouldn't appreciate and reward such personalized treatment. Have you?

And there's another bottom-line-boosting benefit involved. Once you commit to enhancing your selling to women skills, you'll have become a lifelong learner when it comes to customer differences and customer needs. In practicing that approach, you'll develop the ability to get to the top of your game faster. Once you're willing and ready, you'll be able to listen, hear, adapt in the sales process more rapidly and naturally. You will get up to speed with all kinds of target markets more effectively. In short, the process it takes to increase your business among women can also enable you to more readily provide an enhanced experience for all your customers, regardless of who they are.

That's target selling. Once you acquire some selling-to-women skills, you'll be better able to start putting yourself on your customer's wavelength—*any* customer's wavelength. You'll be better able to adapt effectively to new territories, new jobs, new products, new customers, new conditions. That versatility will help you get in sync with almost any kind of customer and stay in step with a U.S. economy increasingly defined by diversity.

With the skills you'll get to sell more in the women's market, you can also do well and do right by all kinds of customers today—and tomorrow. And here's a great irony of it all: By moving beyond the all-male sales model of old, you'll have what it takes to triumph in that game, too, and win big.

chapter two

Getting It, Part I

Understanding Gender Talk

Does this sound familiar?

Jim is a young insurance salesman who often makes cold calls to drum up new business. This puts him on mother's hours—it's a woman who usually answers his calls during the day. One day during calling, he got Janice, a stay-at-home mom with three kids. The family had managed to sock away a modest savings cushion in case of emergency. Lately, she had been thinking seriously about buying some life insurance. Maybe they needed insurance just for her husband, maybe for them both. She was interested, and willing to talk when Jim called.

Jim politely introduced himself, complimented her on her wise planning in wanting to buy life insurance, then began his standard sales pitch. These sales points had paid off plenty of times before, so he worked them one by one with confidence. He talked his talk.

But then Janice talked—and, to Jim, her talk seemed pointless. To him, she took to rambling. First, she told Jim about her children, then about what a tightwad her husband's boss was, then she subjected him to her frustrations about finding a decent job when she returned to the paid workforce because nobody respected the skills it takes to raise kids. Then she veered even farther off course. She spiraled into stories about friends and neighbors, touching down on points like her sister's insurance coverage, her brother-in-law's business, her nephews in private school versus her kids who went to public.

Jim wondered where she was coming from . . . and where she was going. But he had put a lot of time into her and wasn't going to lose out now. He figured her rambling was the result of worry for the future, or some more general insecurity maybe. While she was talking, he began to think of how to redirect her attention to his agenda. When he thought he had a way, he interrupted her.

Jim told Janice, never fear, that he knew exactly what she should do. He had the solution she needed. Then he guided her back on track, picking up again with his prepared script. He fortified this fix with actuarial numbers. He tried to overcome Janice's resistance by telling her he was the top dog in his division and he knew his stuff. He would not steer her wrong.

After ten minutes of that, Janice thanked him for calling but said she had to pick the kids up at school. The truth was she had lost interest. Jim was frustrated. Had she suddenly decided against life insurance in the middle of his best pitch? What was her problem? He chalked it up to a preoccupied woman who couldn't make a decision. Not worth the effort. Move on to the next prospect.

Janice was frustrated, too. She had wanted to buy life insurance, but she felt Jim didn't understand her family concerns and so he was not the right advisor. How could she trust him to recommend the right insurance policy when he couldn't even keep up with the conversation?

The moral of this story: Talk is definitely not cheap. It isn't easy either. *Men and women do it differently, expect different things from it, even hear different things in it. Women tend to multitask in their thinking—and that comes out in their talk.* Men tend to be more focused. They like to stay on track. The styles are different enough that each may think the other is missing the point! The trick is to "get" both styles and touch base where you need to. Otherwise, a lot less will get done, decided—or sold.

What Is She Talking About?

Some experts say men and women are just so different in conversation that there's got to be biology involved. They say different brainwaves are to blame, and science may be beginning to back them up. Brain-mapping technologies are showing some differences in how men and women process information. Still, brains are made to be altered by the outside world. Experience affects the wiring and how brains do their thing; otherwise, we couldn't learn.

To some extent, the different styles are social adaptations because, over the eons, men and women have had different roles to play in the world. Different needs and different resources have produced different ways of talking, asking, listening, and "reading."

I was fascinated by a television series I saw not long ago about the culture of cavemen. The theory was that cave*men* seemed quite satisfied with limited vocabulary. All they needed to do was communicate simple instructions to coordinate hunting and other physical and protective tasks. For a cave*woman,* however, the roles—and needs—were different. She needed to understand family needs, care for children, and generally develop culture, stories, history, and a means to pass it on as legacy. In short, she was the driver of communication. The simple vocabulary that was adequate for a caveman was insufficient for a cavewoman. Some things never change. Research shows that women use more words than men to communicate, they like to tell stories, they tend to leave longer messages, and they tend to explain things in greater detail.

Whatever you make of the various theories to explain the causes of the conversation clash, the good news is, there is a cure. You can learn to talk to a woman—and it won't require rewiring your brain—just by making a few smart moves.

It's called code switching. It's not a 007 thing. You don't need a sharkskin suit or a martini (shaken, not stirred). You don't even need that cool, Bond control. All you need is a clue or two about a woman's way of talking and the smarts to put them into play.

With some customers, it'll be a quick shifting back and forth from a more direct "masculine" talk to a more subtle, emotion-rich "feminine" style. With others, it'll be shifting to her style and staying there. The fact is every woman will show some combination of characteristically feminine and not-so-feminine styles. It varies on an individual basis, from one woman to the next. There are also different tendencies that separate, for example, head-of-household women consumers from women business owners or women corporate executives. To sell well to all, you'll need a range of options—and the ability to deploy them as the situation demands.

Conversational Styles 101

Code switching means changing your speech style to suit the customer you're talking to. To do it well, you've got to understand a woman's conversational style and get a handle on yours, too.

Want to know what women say about the way men talk to them? Get ready, because it isn't pretty. According to the women I've talked to, salesmen seem:

- Too aggressive
- Too pushy
- High pressure
- In a hurry
- Overbearing
- Condescending
- Devious
- To not give you time to think the sale through
- To act superior
- To have too much ego
- To lack patience
- To lack listening skills
- To lack manners

Surprised? Many men are. That's because they don't see their own communication style as a style. They just see it as talking. Or, in this case, as selling. Men aren't taught to think of themselves as a particular group of people; men are taught to think of themselves as "The People." Without ever realizing it, men have been raised to think of themselves as the standard—as typical; as the universal person. But now we know there is no such thing. With the changing demographics of women and diversity today, we've finally realized that "Everyman" isn't "Everybody."

When women balk at men's talk, they are not being oversensitive or hypercritical or "feminazis." And men aren't usually trying to dominate or intimidate or be rude. It just sometimes comes across that way to women because their styles can be so different.

Now let's look at it another way. When women sell to men, or even to other women, they seem:

- To lack product knowledge
- To lack technical knowledge
- Unsure of specifics
- Too emotional
- Too tentative

- Too uncertain
- Too vague
- Unable to make a sound recommendation
- Unable to get to the bottom line

What causes this disconnect? Here's the deal: In general, men talk to compete and to achieve. Men talk to make a point. Men talk to solve problems. It's about logic, efficiency, getting to a goal. It's about facts and actions. Men's talk is take-charge talk. It is decision-making talk. It is the language of people who have been in control of the world and who have been in the position not to worry very much about who might be offended by their style.

On the other hand, women talk to collaborate. Women talk to connect. Women talk to share. Their talk tends to be indirect and subtle. It's about context, feelings, needs. Women's talk is more detailed, less decisive. It's more personal. It uses more stories, more finesse, more nonverbal cues, such as gestures and tone of voice. It is the language of people who have had to survive and grow without much control over their physical, social, or economic world.

figure 2.1   How We Buy

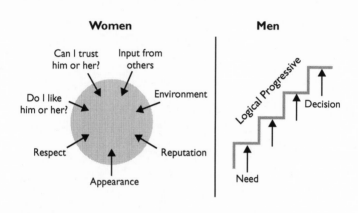

Buying styles follow from these different communication styles (see Figure 2.1).

The culture clash seems clear. Men connect with other men through competition. They talk to show or express independence, rank, and superiority. They move logically toward a goal, toward the top, toward some kind of victory. Women connect with other women to show or express commonality, empathy, and understanding. They move more circularly, forming trust, understanding, and a relationship. *The two styles can be at cross purposes: Achieve versus connect. Compete versus collaborate. Goals versus needs.*

Directness versus details. No wonder what we often get is frustration, miscommunication, and distrust. No wonder women feel men lack patience, don't listen, and have no manners. Men's talk often aims at scoring, winning, or impressing people, which isn't what women are in it for. No wonder when women complain of pushy, aggressive, or high-pressure tactics: most men don't see it. In fact, men would like a little more action, direction, and decisiveness, thank you very much. That's how men get the job done without getting lost "in the details."

The "And" Factor

It's not that women are incapable of straight talk. It's that women have been the keepers of family culture and relationships, which are maintained by spinning words, talk, and stories. They have had to evolve subtle ways to get their needs met without making listeners angry.

Evolution is constant; it is always going on. As women become more empowered in the world, their talk is changing. It's already apparent with women business owners and women executives. In my experience, they tend to be more direct, more to-the-point in purchasing. Why? For one thing, they are time-starved from the double day that most working women face. They don't have time to waste in the process of shopping or in getting what they decide to buy up and running.

Another reason men tend to be more direct is because they can. Research shows that styles of talk relate to levels of power. Less powerful people tend to use some elements of "women's talk," regardless of sex; more powerful people use bits of "men's talk," regardless of sex. These tendencies apply across racial and ethnic groups, too. Businesswomen and professionals of color are becoming aware that they have the power to make decisions and worry less than others might about how those decisions are received.

Taken together, I call this the "'And' Factor." Some women customers today use traditional "feminine" speech styles *AND* traditional "masculine" speech styles in nearly equal measure. High-powered women such as executives and business owners have learned to use the masculine style to be respected and effective in the workplace—where goal orientation, competitivenss, and directness are needed to get the job done. Yet they also maintain more feminine patterns—which they bring to their work and purchasing power as an additive. As an "And." Some women—especially those with businesses, careers, and big purchasing power—now talk the way men have traditionally talked *AND* they still talk like women have traditionally talked.

It seems as though age-old habits die hard. Besides, people who have power in the workplace still may not have it so much at home or in the street. While a lot has changed for women, as well as diversity customers, many things are still much the same. So, no matter how senior or successful they are, businesswomen, and all those who have historically lacked power, will still talk the traditional talk in some ways and to some degree.

Talking the Talk

Think of women's talk as a dialect. It's like a version of the dominant standard, which would be men's talk. And it is widespread. Similar forms exist, with some differences, in almost every culture on the planet. This may be due to biology or social history. It's also a hard fact of history that women have faced similar social conditions and constraints just about everywhere in the world.

Let's map it out. Here are the top ten traits in women's talk worldwide:

1. Women tend to use more expressive words, more adjectives than nouns or verbs.
2. Women tend to be more indirect.
3. Women's talk tends to be more collaborative and less competitive.
4. Women tend to use more "emotion" words.
5. Women's intonation patterns at times resemble questions.
6. Women tend to hedge more in conversation.
7. Women tend to use more nonverbal cues.
8. Women may take longer to commit themselves to an opinion.
9. Women tend to use better grammar and less jargon.
10. Women tend to use more words that convey imprecise quantities, like "so" or "such."

OK, most of these may seem small, but taken together they make all the difference in the world. In reality, there are "big picture" issues, such as the first four; there are midsized elements, such as the next four; and there are finer points of interest, such as those that end the list.

What all this adds up to off the top is you've got to ditch your prepared pitch—which you probably wrote with men customers in mind, whether you were aware of it or not.

But you won't be going in bare. Parts of your script, presented in the right way and at the right time, may still do the trick. The thing is, you won't be able to run it like clockwork. You'll have to break it down to its nuts and bolts so you can think through the code-switching cues that will make it make better sense to a woman.

It's not that hard to retool your talk for better performance with women. Let's look at it one step at a time.

Use Adjectives in Your Talk

You'll want to use adjectives in your conversation. They build rapport because women tend to be more descriptive in their speech than men. So brush up on some. (Adjectives are words that describe nouns;

they are words that describe things, rather than actions.) Take note of the adjectives your female customers use to describe things. That will give you a field guide, pre-tested for your demographics, ready to put into use. Your list may become long—but the longer the list, the more agile you'll be at talking to different customers.

Be Patient

Women are more expansive and less direct than men; they may tend to hedge; they tend to be less committal and are more imprecise about sizes, quantities, distances. This kind of talk can make men bail—but that will never close a sale. Patience will. You *can* deal. If a woman has been talking on and on, you may find yourself talking over her because you thought she was done, but she wasn't. Instead, try this: When you think she is finished speaking, count to four before you begin to respond or move on. If you find your mind wandering while she searches for her true point, there are active listening techniques, detailed in Chapter 3, to help you stay with her.

Collaborate

Women's talk is collaborative while men's talk is competitive. Huh? What does that mean? Bottom line, it means women tend to involve more people in decision making and want more input from friends and family. Men are taught it is manly to go it alone, to make their decisions for themselves. They see asking around as a sign of insecurity or ineptitude. But it's not. It's a means evolved—just like men's style—to serve a different set of ends. Below are simple techniques you can use to signal a more open style that women will relate to:

- Use both pronouns—him and her, his and hers—alternatively. Don't always use one or the other when talking about general tendencies or situations.
- Cite the input of others when describing products, services, or your own evaluation process. Quote them. Include their stories. This both humanizes you and your selling, and includes your client.
- Be ready to share references of friends and family members, or of other women customers.

This shows your business is woman-friendly and underscores why: because you are caring, forthcoming, and involved.

Don't Fix a Problem—Express a Feeling

Women complain that men are overbearing in the sales process and too often tell them what to do. This is a massive issue for them. Over and over again, women say men talk to instantly fix or solve things—and women don't want to hear that. To make a point with a woman, couch it in a feeling: "I sense that you're ready for a bigger system." "I see that you're frustrated by the complicated controls on this machine." This will help her connect with you—and your solution.

Use Emotion Words

Women's talk is more attuned to emotions, relationships, context; men's to facts, data, status. To make a better connection, use more emotion and feeling words. Make a list. You can start with these winners.

On the upside:

- Devoted
- Committed
- Pleased
- Delighted

On the downside:

- Concerned
- Upset
- Frustrated
- Angry

But don't go crazy. Too many emotion words will sound phony to her. As a general rule, use no more than three or four throughout a half-hour conversation. To prevent going overboard, just focus on her style. If she uses a lot of emotion words herself, she may be comfortable with more from you. If she's nodding along, supporting your talk, but suddenly stops, you've lost her. To regain your footing, drop out or drop down the emotional intensity.

Use Formality To Bring You Closer

Women tend to be more correct and formal in their speech than men. This makes sense because women have had to be careful to appear correct and proper, especially in public, lest they pay a price meted out by most societies against "loose" talk or "loose" women. So straighten up. Avoid slang, which may be insulting to some female customers. Lose or scale back the industry jargon. Men might think their tech talk or a battalion of stats is an impressive show of mastery, and it might be to other men, but women often find it arrogant and obnoxious. Too often, it puts them off. Instead, impress her with some polite phrasing and respectful attention.

Walking the Talk

Mark, a young investment broker at a major firm, learned what women want the hard way. In meeting with a well-established couple in their 40s, he presumed that the husband was as in charge as he was talkative, and that the wife was more quiet—and acquiescent—by nature. He talked his top-tier talk, and felt he had pitched their business well. Days later he hadn't heard from them. When Mark finally reached the husband, he was told they chose not to use his services. Mark didn't get it and wondered what went wrong.

The wife, it turned out, did not get the attention from him that she expected. While Mark had good intentions, his gender assumptions and lack of gender awareness together sunk the sale. For starters, Mark had talked mainly to the husband. He should have at least given the wife something closer to equal treatment in conversation. Beyond that, Mark should have known that her perceptions of equal attention might well be different than his. Women tend to talk more and to value talk differently than men do. Why wouldn't that affect their expectations in this conversation, too?

Sounds complicated, but when it comes to negotiating and selling, what women want is actually pretty simple. In fact, it's a lot less than you're probably doing now. They don't want to be ignored, given short shrift, talked down to, or told what to think or what to buy. What they want is to be partners in conversation; to be shown things eye to eye. What most women customers want is to be invited in, then met at least half way. Probably more—but make sure you do give her no less.

It's called "parity." It means sufficient attention and opportunity in conversation, sufficient access to the floor. Parity demonstrates power. More powerful people get the floor; less powerful people listen, watch, and wait.

In mixed conversation, research shows a woman typically gets less talk time and less attention time than a man—even if she outranks him. That's not fair but, more to the point here, it's really not good. Because women are typically more expansive, they are going to need more talk than a man would before they feel they've said what they want to say.

So what can you do? *Structure talk in her terms. Go beyond even equal time and get to parity. Offer a woman customer a woman-sized share of the floor time.* Everyone will be different, but ball park: Give a woman a 20 percent premium on talk time—that is, 20 percent more than you would give a man in the same situation.

We also judge parity by eye contact, and female customers are particularly keen on it. In selling to couples, I've found a good guideline is a 60/40 split, with the larger share of eye contact going to the woman. If it's one-on-one, it's never polite to stare, but be sure your eyes don't wander from her or flit away with every background sound or passerby. Focus your eyes on her and your attention will follow. Most important, if you look at only her when she's talking, she'll feel valued, she'll feel respected, she'll feel heard. And that's what the vast majority of women customers need before they decide to buy.

Gender parity is most often torpedoed by interruption. Research shows that men routinely interrupt women in conversation and don't think twice or make room once they've taken the floor. In negotiating and selling, women say too many men "mind read." They decide in no time that they have all the answers, even if the woman hasn't finished asking the questions yet. They interrupt, then drive ahead to the finish line, telling and selling the solution without looking back. There is almost nothing that will more quickly sour or sink a potential sale. Luckily, there is something you can do about it.

If you have the urge to interrupt, that means you're more focused mentally on what you're thinking than on what's she's saying. Recognize this and refocus on her. Try these two tricks:

1. *Take notes.* Writing down points she's making will keep you focused on her needs and help you see what she will need to proceed.
2. *Take five.* When she's finished speaking, take five seconds to review your notes. The delay will come in handy in case she needs to share more, and will allow you to think about what she has just said to continue with her needs in mind.

Remember, when you're talking about difference, equal treatment will not mean same treatment. If you treat a woman customer the same way you'd treat a man, she won't feel respected. She won't feel equal or included. In fact, she'll probably feel disregarded, pushed aside, and maybe even insulted. Instead, think parity. You want to adjust, to code switch, to retool your talk to give any and all customers their fair share in their own terms. Because parity reflects power, achieving it in conversation makes you a team. That's something customers, not just women, want when they are buying, especially when they are buying big.

(chapter three)

Getting It, Part II
Listening Techniques That
Get Through

We've all been there. A woman walks into your sales territory looking like a strong prospect. She's confident, motivated, so you figure she's a woman with the authority to say yes and sign off. You walk up to her and ask if you can help her with something today. She nods, and then starts talking.

She tells you about how her old whatever you're selling—copier, computer, car—failed her when she needed it most. She was stranded. She's still furious. She adds that it was a disappointment anyway; it never did what she wanted from day one. They just don't make things the way they should, she continues. Her best friend spent a fortune on a top-of-the-line machine by a close competitor, but that was a waste of money. It was stocked with bells and whistles, but these were just confusing. Next, out of the blue, she says her budget is up in the air because her home is being renovated, her husband has been sick, and she's got two kids, one packing for college next year.

By this time, you've lost track of what she is talking about, are probably bored, and would just like the facts. You're ready to bail.

Myth: She's unsure about what she wants and unable to make a decision.

Reality: There's a reason to her rhyme. You've just got to figure out how to follow it. You've got to learn how to listen her way.

A woman's way of communicating is definitely different from a man's. Maybe it's disorienting at first, but it's not rocket science. You're not on another planet. You just need to adjust to the changed terrain Nobody questions the smarts of an MLB outfielder who adjusts his own position because a batter shifts his leg an inch or two forward or back. That's what you need to do: Understand her style and make informed adjustments to your moves, because that's what it takes to win.

Remember: Men communicate to get somewhere. Talk is a tool, a way to compete, a means to a goal. Listening is, too. When he listens, he does it to achieve results: solve the problem, win the argument, get the last laugh, finish the job, close the deal.

With women, the process may seem more ad hoc by comparison. Certainly, it is much less to the point. Talk is a process of discovery, a journey, or maybe it's even therapy. Women ask a billion questions. They tend to think out loud. They explore. Some women only realize where they're coming from by talking it through. That's just how they do it. Know it. Accept it. Adjust.

There's another thing you need to know to listen to women well: Women listen to plenty of people before they'll ink a deal. *Men are trained to decide for themselves. They fear it's weak to seek advice. Women don't see it that way. They decide differently. They include others. They consult. It's fair to say, on some level, women buy by consensus.*

This makes men frustrated, discouraged—or even furious. But lighten up: Just because a woman doesn't talk or decide to buy like a man would doesn't mean she can't make a decision or won't buy big when she does. It's best to ignore the voice in your head that says she is playing control games with you. She is not toying with you by *not knowing,* by passivity, by passing the buck to unseen people beyond your reach. Actually, she's being honest. She's just being herself. This is normal for her. Appreciate it. Accept it. Adjust.

Most women say nobody listens to them. To some extent, this is literally true. Research on cross-sex conversation routinely finds that men introduce most of the "successful" topics and are supported by women in keeping that subject alive. That means, much of the time, men talk and women listen. This pattern holds no matter where or who a woman is. Even a woman who outranks a man—a woman executive, a woman business owner, a woman principal, a stay-at-home mom employing someone to do work in the house, you name it—very often finds herself expected to be the polite listener, not the take-charge talker.

But there's even more to it than that. When a woman says nobody listens to her, what she also means is she doesn't feel *heard.* She doesn't feel understood. Style differences can be so major that many men tell me they struggle to stay with women when they talk. To them, the woman veers off topic and their minds wander or they just don't get where she's going.

Admit it: If you're not listening to a woman customer it's probably because: (1) you assume you already understand her requirements so you can block out what she's saying; or (2) you're focused on your own agenda, which pulls you away and makes it that much tougher to make heads or tails of her talk.

Whatever the reason, women tend to have finer-tuned social perceptions than men, so they usually notice if you're moving away or have logged off. Once she senses this, it will often lead to frustration and doubts about your ability to meet her needs.

The upside is that the fix is fairly easy: Don't interrupt. Don't "mind read" her needs. Don't try to solve all her problems. Don't expect her to get with the program. Just stay calm and let her lead the conversation. Refocus on whatever it is that she is putting out there. Your job is to be ready, willing, and able to adjust your footing to field her. You'll be very glad you did, because when a woman believes you are there, that you really hear her, you might just get her business for life—and that of her friends and family, too.

Listen Up: Getting the Information You Need

So what's the next step? What can you do with the female customer like the one who opened this chapter? For starters, you can tune into her vibe. Even hard-nosed businesswomen are raised to make a priority of relationships, needs, feelings, and people. Those are the notes to follow.

In the opening example, the woman started by telling you she felt stranded when her old machine failed her. She'll feel heard if you address this *feeling*. When the time comes to talk options, tell her about your product's reliability and warranty, and let her know what will safeguard her from ever feeling stranded again.

She also said too many features and too much hype were intimidating. You should recognize that she won't respond well to a hard sell—because that will make you and your products seem untrustworthy. Also, this customer will probably be impressed by simple value, by a machine that doesn't promise her the moon but will actually do everything it promises. Tell her that the sense of trustworthiness—the *feeling* you now know she is after—is why you want to show her the products that you do.

A budget crunch is always critical sales info, but in this case even better information is available between the lines. Think people. Think relationships. For starters, that means you've got to get the cast of characters straight. If you don't remember names, at least get relationships—"mother," "husband," "son," "sister-in-law," or whatever it may be.

Next, you should follow the feelings. Her reasons for watching the price tag tell you this is one busy woman—a working mom who right now has pressure to perform financially in her business and be an extra caring wife to a sick spouse. Her house is under construction, which can be very disruptive and there is lots to decide. Her kids are growing up, moving on, which is a big change and a new chapter in her life. Imagine how impressed she'll be if you can relate your product to reducing her stress, simplifying her life, and helping her to manage and maintain the normal. Hear her need for product efficiency and high performance in light of her full plate. If you deliver the value proposition from that standpoint, she's almost sure to feel the fit.

So, to recap:

■ *Think feelings.* A woman's feelings are often part of her thoughts. She's not as compartmentalized as your average man—and that's a crucial linkage. If she tells you a product made her feel good, go with that: Show how yours is similar in that way. If you hear that a product made her feel bad, shift into reverse: Show how yours is different. Listen to her feeling words, emotional states, and loaded terms—*stranded, furious, disappointment, confusing, scam.* These are the signposts that tell you where she is coming from—and where you should go.

■ *Think relationships.* She does. Be on the same wavelength with that. Don't try to impress her with facts and figures—on their own and out of context, this will probably backfire. Relate your product or service to the people in her life. (You've been listening, so you know who they are.) Will the TV's high sound quality be especially good for her 74-year-old mother? Will the easy fold-down of the SUV's seating make carpooling a cinch? Put products in place with people. That will help her really see their value.

- *Think context.* Sure, you're selling products and services to what she needs to get done. But to seal the deal, sell to what she needs to make her life better. The 24/7 economy is bearing down on everybody, but women carry a double load on their backs. They are stressing to work their way up in the world while still putting in most of the "second shift"—the cleanup, catering, and kid planning—at home. These days, the pressure is on to be good in both places. If you can speak to her life, sell to be a positive part of it—and she'll probably buy from you again and again.

Show Her You're Listening

Men especially like to *do things*. Well, there are things a salesperson can do to blow the sale—like talk too much, talk too soon, try to fix things, push too hard—and things he or she can do to bring in her business for life. The first thing to do with women customers is to make them feel heard whenever you can. Even the perception that you're listening is a start.

It's called "responsive listening." This is what a woman will do with another woman to express, "I'm there," "I'm with you." It's great for men because it gives them something to *do* while listening—to keep them from doing the wrong things they might want to do, such as interrupt or jump the gun to the solution before she's finished explaining the situation.

It's easy, and it works. For starters, use simple, supportive gestures, such as smiling or nodding every once in a while. This lets her know that you are there with her, taking time and taking it in. It also sends a second crucial message: approval. Research shows approving gestures help everyone open up, and if a woman is looking for reassurance, this will help her get it.

You should be sure to use some reassuring phrases in your conversation. Sure bets include:

- "If I understand you correctly . . ."
- "That's interesting, tell me more."
- "I see."

- "Go on."
- "What else?"

When there's a pause, or if she says something part way, throw out one of these phrases. If she says her current car always seems cluttered or is really hard to park or her kids get sweaty or chilly in the back seat, use supportive phrases to keep her talking and help push her to the point.

Even the simplest acknowledgment will go a long way to show your average woman you are following her—or at least making the effort. She'll like your attentiveness with the occasional:

- "Hmm . . ."
- "Uh-huh."
- "OK."

Paraphrasing is another no-sweat technique that delivers stellar returns. Some people may think it's just restating the obvious; after all, what could be more obvious than what she just said? But women feel reassured and supported when they know you are really listening, and paraphrasing is an easy way to prove it to them. In addition, restating the main points helps you make sure you are really getting the picture. It's a no-brainer that provides a big mental boost: It prevents the all-too-common tune out, because the one thing paraphrasing demands is attention to exactly what she is saying.

A cousin of paraphrasing—if perhaps a poor relation—is the echo technique. All you do is repeat the last few words of whatever she tells you. So, if she says she's buying a home in Florida, you echo back, "Oh, so you're buying a home in Florida . . ." If she says she's unhappy with her computer monitor, you repeat back to her, "I see, so you're not happy with your current monitor . . ." It's more effective if you put some emphasis behind the object of her sentence. The echo technique is simple, but it can help her feel heard. Just be careful not to overuse it. At some point, some people can feel insulted or mocked by it.

Remember that women typically buy by consensus, and that they talk along those lines, too. Believe it or not, they even want the people they purchase from to be part of their team. *But nobody likes to be told what to do. Women especially don't like it when men swing in and want to solve all their problems. So be a collaborator. Instead of fixing and solving, just jump in on her side.* Be sure to use phrases that say, "I'm open for input from others"—starting with her. Try:

- "Let me make sure I understand you."
- "What I hear is . . ."
- "It seems to me that . . ."
- "It could be that . . ."
- "It looks to me like . . ."
- "It sounds to me like . . ."
- "I feel as though . . ."
- "Am I right?"

These phrases help position you as part of her team, and also get you confirmation on whatever you want to know.

Accept, Adjust, Win

The thing that torpedoes most cross-sex negotiating and selling is not so much gender differences in style—confusing and frustrating as some may find them to be. It's what happens next, especially for men. I've seen problems stemming from what men *do* with their reactions. Too often, when a man doesn't understand a woman's point of view, he disconnects. Sometimes he gets angry or confused and frustrated. A blame game sets in, and his confusion and frustration combust. When the smoke clears, the woman customer has become the target of contempt.

There is nothing—repeat: nothing—a salesperson can do that will more quickly derail the sale than to talk down to a woman. Nobody likes to be talked down to, but women today are especially sensitive to that. Luckily, there are simple things a salesperson can do to avoid this downfall, such as:

- Decide to let her lead the conversation.
- Choose to explore, not explain.
- Practice not saying anything that sounds like you've got the fix.
- Tell her if you don't understand what she's saying and ask her to clarify.
- Allow her to ask any and all questions.
- Accept her tendency to include feelings in her thinking.
- If you want to suggest a different approach, rephrase her point before voicing yours.

The bottom line: To deal well with women customers and clients, you cannot capitulate to frustration. It closes communication and makes selling much tougher. Her way is her way, and by now you know that means "different." Not better or worse, but different. And guess what: Not all men are alike either. The winners today are those who can take that in stride—then run with it.

chapter four

Taking the Field

Ten Steps to Building the Relationship

What motivates a woman to buy? Top of the list is her relationship with the salesperson. It is the point of connection that will drive the sale. How comfortable will you make her feel? Are you sensitive and caring? Are you a good listener? Can she trust you?

Sound familiar? This is what matters to women in many types of relationships, including the sales relationship. Men are transaction-focused as customers, but for women, it's all about connection and trust (see Figure 4.1).

figure 4.1   How Women Buy

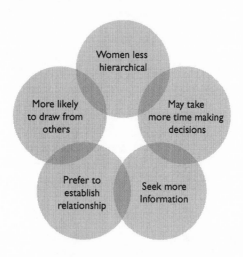

As familiar as all this might be, if you get frustrated when it comes to relating to women customers, you're not alone. I hear every day how much harder it is to close a woman than a man. Some clients tell me their sales force draws straws to see who has to wait on the woman customer who just walked in the door. Why? Because she'll probably ask a million questions, take up your time on tangents, maybe get offended at something, and ultimately fail to buy. She'll say she has "to think about it."

Yet creating a relationship that works with women is actually not that hard to do. It's like learning to dance: You just have to know what steps to take. Here's a simple ten-point program for connecting with woman customers:

1. Welcome her with a handshake and a smile.
2. Give her your card.
3. Create the right environment.
4. Make eye contact.
5. Let her take the lead.
6. Listen attentively.
7. Listen attentively some more.
8. Ask the right questions.
9. Empower her.
10. Go for her comfort zone.

Let's just take it one step at a time.

1. Welcome Her with a Handshake and a Smile

Buy-in begins with "Hello," so be sure to give a woman a proper welcome. Are you pleased to meet her? (Right answer: Yes.) Then show it: Smile, look her in the eye, and shake her hand.

You'd be surprised how many women tell me they are turned off from the get-go by a bad handshake. They want one that says, "I regard you as an equal," "I respect you as a decision maker." Too often, from men and women, they get an overpowering one that says, "I've got your situation under control," or a careless one that says, "Do I have to even bother?"

A good handshake technique can change your life, and I've had many a salesperson tell me so. It gets things going on the right track, and you need that to make headway with women.

Review your own handshake style and ask yourself:

- Does your hand sit solidly *in* her hand—not all over it, or part way there? (Some customers are OK with the other hand folded over in a handshake, but only if it's genuine, and even then, if you can sense that she'll be comfortable with it. When in doubt, don't do it.)

- Does the base between your thumb and index finger fit comfortably with hers? You shouldn't shake her fingertips.

- Do you hold her hand firmly, but not too tight? Squeezing can make you come off as grasping or insensitive.

- Do you shake earnestly and confidently, but moderately? It's hard to have confidence in someone who has a wimpy handshake, and no one—especially no woman customer—likes to feel overpowered.

2. Give Her Your Card

Women prefer more formality than men do, especially in cross-sex situations. When selling to women remember that they like politeness, and be sure to formally introduce yourself.

When you approach a female customer, say your name when you first say hello. As soon as the ice is broken and you are settling into selling conversation, give her your card as well. If she's with a partner, give both a card.

Never assume only one is the decision maker who needs to know your name. That could be misinterpreted—and it could cost you the sale. Recently a colleague of mine, a woman business owner in her 40s, went with her regional manager, a man in his late 30s, to meet with a banker about some lending business. The manager was given a card, but the business owner wasn't. Unfortunately for him, the banker assumed that the man was the manager, and, of course, that he ran the show. She was furious at the insult—and rightly so. As it turned out, she was the owner of a multimillion-dollar services company and, as a result, the banker lost out on a substantial account.

Make sure you use her name throughout your conversation, but be careful not to overdo it. When you think a point is particularly important or strongly relevant to her situation, using her name can call attention to these important factors. In general, saying her name not only shows that you are making the effort to reach out to her; it also helps establish and reinforce the sense of cooperation in the selling process that helps women ink the deal.

3. Create the Right Environment

Your office or selling space should reflect you as a professional, organized, and attentive person she can talk to. With women, you want everything about you to express your credibility, your integrity, and your consideration for her needs. She will buy from you when she feels she can trust you, that you are on her side—and your selling environment can go a long way to help those feelings along or to alienate her before you get to say a single word.

Women are affected and their judgment is skewed by environment, so do sweat the details. A space that's neat, clean, and organized is somewhat more important to women than to men. You should sit down to talk, and there should be at least two chairs, preferably around a table instead of across a desk. Family photos are a nice touch. Also keep in mind that women notice everything, including dirt or ink on your hands, that missing sleeve or collar button, or those small stains on your tie that you thought would go unnoticed.

4. Make Eye Contact

Women have learned over the eons to tune in to body language, but the same signals can mean different things to men and women.

When men deal with other men, direct eye contact can be interpreted as a challenge. It can up the ante in a competition-like negotiation process. Some men tell me they typically downplay direct eye contact when dealing with other men—even their friends.

On the other hand, women value eye contact as a sign of respect and connection. The *lack* of eye contact can make them feel insulted or ignored. Or, they interpret it as evasive or shifty. To gain her trust, and thus her business, you must meet her eye to eye.

5. Let Her Take the Lead

Research shows that, in conversation, the person with higher status holds the floor—talks more often, talks longer, launches more "successful" topics. Think of you and your boss—your boss gets the floor. Think of you and your kids—you get it (unless they are teenagers, when everything generally goes out the window—or the door). In mixed conversation, the person who holds the floor is almost always the man, regardless of rank. That means, in general, men usually get to do most of the talking, and women most of the listening, even if the woman is higher on the totem pole or the guest list.

Whatever women feel about these silent structures in their personal lives, they don't like them in the selling process, where status should go to the customer, male or female. The customer may not always be right, but he or she should always get the floor.

So just do it. Give it to her, and let her do the talking. A general rule you should follow: Let her talk about 75 percent of the time at the start. (If time limits work better for you, keep your own talking time to no more than one minute. After that, you need her conversational go-ahead to say more.)

Let her define the problem. Give her what she wants rather than trying to convince her otherwise. That's one of the first, best ways you can show the respect and consideration she needs to buy. It doesn't take much from you, and it will mean a lot to her. The pattern of being denied the floor is so pervasive in women's lives that she'll surely notice the difference.

Men tend to like to fix things. They may think they know what her business or her family needs are, and they may even be right. Even so, that won't make the sale—and it could break it. Most women customers are a lot less likely to buy if you tell them to. Instead, allow a woman customer to take the lead in the decision-making process. Work with her to resolve issues by recommending products or services, and allow her to recognize how these recommendations will provide her value on her own terms.

6. Listen Attentively

Women appreciate people who take the time to let them talk; people who not only let them share their thoughts and concerns, but also allow them to keep talking until they feel they've gotten their point across. I can't tell you how many times women have complained to me that salespeople just don't listen, that they just don't understand.

Unfortunately, many men presume they understand a woman's requirements and tend to block out what she's saying. Or, they interrupt her, saying something like, "I know exactly the product you need," without allowing her to explain her thoughts completely. This is one reason many women say male salespeople are often pushy, aggressive, condescending, or superior. Even more say salespeople lack patience, listening skills, and manners. These feelings from women customers clearly are not conducive to success. Thus, common listening problems can often sink the sale.

So when she's talking, listen up. She's the customer. Her style may be different, and more of her feelings may be involved in the purchasing process than are part of the equation with men. While you may feel a woman may embellish or expand more than a man would, it's best to be patient. In other words, become an enlightened man. If you can't, then at least don't interrupt, let her lead the conversation as much as possible, and let her ask you questions that seem relevant to her. When she does, you can seize the moment: Answer them as effectively and fully as you possibly can.

7. Listen Attentively Some More

I always tell people, the first winning strategy for selling to women is: Listen, listen, and listen some more. There's a reason we are given two ears and one mouth—so we can do twice as much listening!

Careful listening is a true sign of respect for women. But it isn't easy, especially for men. Men like to *do* things. Anybody with a busy schedule may find it difficult to listen well to a woman's expansive talk. Luckily, there are things you can do to help you listen longer, listen better, and show her you care (see the active listening techniques in Chapter 3).

8. Ask the Right Questions

With women customers, you want to have them talking and keep yourself listening—but with a purpose. You need to know what you need to know to sell your product or service, and that means asking the right questions in the right way when you get the chance.

Off the top, you want to ask open-ended questions that create a dialogue. That means questions that start with the proverbial who, what, when, where, and why. They are meant to give you information, and also to build rapport.

When you need more specifics, be sure you ask questions in a nonconfrontational way. Allow her to share her feelings and speak her mind openly and honestly. The easiest way to do this is to use active listening phrasing, such as the following:

- "Let me make sure I'm understanding you. Are you saying that . . . ?"
- "Am I hearing you say that . . . ?"
- "I'm not sure if I know what you mean. Could you tell me more about . . . ?"
- "It sounds to me like you're concerned about . . . Am I with you on that?"

With women customers, remember even the best-crafted questions will get at what she's looking for *in context*. That's the position from which you'll need to sell. No amount of intelligent questioning will get most women to tell you the features they want in a product or service. Rather, you'll find out what problems she wants to solve or what she wants to happen that isn't happening now or what risks she wants to reduce or remove. By smart use of more targeted questions, you may also learn what her decision-making criteria are and who is involved in the decision-making process.

9. Empower Her

Women feel comfortable in making purchasing decisions when they feel empowered by salespeople to decide well. So be prepared with plenty of information, both written and oral. Women especially like to have written information they can refer to over time.

Be careful to avoid the impulse to impress her with a lot of facts and figures. She probably won't respond to reams of data, even if they show good results. Instead, use sales calls to educate her on the products and services she inquires about and on the ones you recommend. Never just tell her a product or service is not right for her. Rather, explain to her how that product or service works and why you recommend against it. By doing this, you will not only involve her in the decision to choose a more appropriate product, you will also have empowered her with the information she needs to better understand and appreciate your other comments and recommendations. In short, you will have educated her to buy better while also enhancing the all-important relationship.

You'll sell well to a woman if you can help her see how the product or service itself can help her. A successful salesperson will be able to understand and articulate the contribution a product or service will make in support of a woman's goals.

10. Go for Her Comfort Zone

Women not only tend to gather more information than men do before they buy, they also like to gather more feedback from others. Input from people a woman trusts and respects will go a long way toward helping her reach her comfort zone—the point at which she will buy.

I once heard a psychologist describe in very visual terms the difference between men and women in the buying process. It went something like this: A man goes into a store to buy a white shirt. He sees a white shirt, it's his size, it's the right fit, and the right blend of cotton. Bingo—he's off to the register. He may think about his purchase afterward but most likely will not. Why should he? He had a task in mind and the task is complete. Move on to the next. In short, think of it in these terms: He sees, he thinks, and then he acts.

On the other hand, it's quite a different experience for women. A women goes into a store looking for a white shirt. She finds a large selection and begins the quest for the *right* white shirt. She tries on several, and while a few would work, they may not be good enough to compel her to buy. Instead, several thoughts race through her brain: "Macy's is having a sale"; "Nordstrom always has such great new styles"; "Maybe I should splurge and get that DKNY shirt that cost a fortune but will look so good with my new suit"; and on and on. So she continues her quest, which at this point may take hours or possibly days, until she feels good enough about her decision to buy.

In short, women need to "feel" a product or service is right before they move forward. A man's buying process is usually see-think-act (sometimes the "think" and the "act" are interchangeable). A woman's process is more like see-think-think some more-feel a purchase is right for her-act. The "feel" part of the equation may be hard to get your head around. It may involve her gathering additional information about what's available or consulting others to gain various points of view. It may just take time for the decision to settle into place and seem right. Whatever it takes, it's crucial for women customers. Usually, a feeling is the clincher for women when it comes to the close.

You can move a woman forward by playing some trigger points within her buying process. Just remember the number-one rule: Don't push the close. Accept that she may not be able to close on the first meeting. It's a good idea to offer her referrals to your other female clients. This can act as a reference for you and a decision-making resource for her. Let her see for herself that you are comfortable and successful working with women like her, and that you have come through for them. She's going to ask around anyway, so bring her into *your* network of satisfied customers to keep the spin going your way. Plus, other women may be able to sing your praises in a language and on a level that they share—and you might never fully be privy to. But as long as you're doing it right, you're golden.

chapter five

Get On Her Team

Positioning That Works

You've heard the old saying, "Perception is everything." Well, I would bet that insight was probably written by a woman. Women tend to notice more details about their surroundings—and they draw important information from these observations. Meanwhile, men, focusing on goals, keep surroundings on the sidelines.

Let me illustrate. I have a client who runs a cruise-ship line. We surveyed men and women customers about their staterooms after a weeklong cruise. The vast majority of women customers noticed every detail, right down to the design of the rugs beneath their feet and the subject of each painting on the walls. In contrast, after a full week, almost none of the men could identify even the color of the paint on the walls. Most couldn't recall the color of the furniture, either. Those details just didn't register for them.

Women see the setting as integral, not peripheral. They develop a picture—actually, more of a collage or mosaic—about you and your business, taking into account a thousand small factors. They are always adding information.

In negotiating and selling, it's the picture that really does speak a thousand words. Because a woman buyer is likely to consult with at least two salespeople before a major purchase, you want to make sure your surroundings "say" the things she needs to hear. Are you telling her you are disorganized, overwhelmed, and lack focus? Or, are you showing her that you are:

- Smart
- Knowledgeable
- Helpful
- Understanding
- Considerate
- Reliable
- Trustworthy

Those are the "indirect" messages you want your surroundings to convey.

Remember, women aren't being picky or difficult when they notice these things. They are just being women instead of men. Think about it: Whatever else a woman may be doing in the world and the workplace, she is still considered to be the keeper of the home, and she is seen as responsible for its quality. Plus, society has always made women more visible. Because they are often being looked at, women put extra time and effort into fashion sense and personal style. Environment and appearance make a difference in their success and happiness; these things matter in their lives.

It's not a big surprise then that women take that mentality with them everywhere they go. When you and your workspace reflect a similar sense of setting, a woman feels you and she see eye to eye—a factor that is crucial for her when it comes time to buy.

Neatness Counts

For a woman, the purchasing experience begins before she ever sets eyes on a salesperson. It starts as she approaches the front door. It continues as she proceeds through your office, showroom, or workspace; it keeps going to your desk and through your conversation. It doesn't end until quite a while after she's out the door and on her way back home or to the office. The impression you make stays with her—and influences how she proceeds.

It's a long haul. From start to finish, however, remember this: Neatness counts. Why? Because neatness suggests competency. Sloppy surroundings send the message that you are not on top of your job, that you don't have a handle on your products or services. It registers poorly on her trust meter. On the other hand, a neat, spiffy workspace says to her "smart," "knowledgeable," "reliable"—and that's right where you want her to be.

That's the ticket with her, so here's how to get on board:

1. Your Office, Showroom, or Workspace

Starting from the front door, you need to think of your office as a reflection of you, because she does. Is the entry clean, safe, well marked, and easy to negotiate? Women face enough obstacles in their every-day lives. They don't need to feel challenged as they enter the purchasing experience or approach you.

Is the waiting area warm and welcoming or worn and cluttered? Are there any magazines or brochures for her to look at? Is there anything that adds color or a sense of attention to the area? How about the first people she sees. Does a receptionist or customer service rep make her feel that everyone is glad she came in?

2. Your Meeting Space

There are two proven setups that do well when doing business with women. Remember these shapes: "round" and "90-degree angle."

A round table with chairs suggests equality and unity. Nobody sits at the head, nobody is the chief, nobody is anointed the talker while the other is relegated to role of listener. Rather, this setup says the conversation is meant to "go around," that everybody is equally positioned for participation. A round table also promotes a sense of collaboration. There's nothing like a circle to bring people together.

A sofa and chair at a 90-degree angle is another good play—if you play it right. She gets the sofa; you take the chair. Never sit on the sofa with her. That's too close for most women's comfort. Besides, if she comes with a partner, or a colleague, or her husband, they should share the communal sofa space.

3. Your Desk

Your desk is the heart of your workspace. Is it ready and waiting to focus on her, or is it in disarray, piled high with distractions and baggage? Keep your desk neat, clean, and ready to do business *with her.* You can handle it. Here's how:

Don't have piles and piles of files and clutter.

Do keep an empty drawer to stow them, if necessary, just until she leaves.

Don't have materials strewn across your desk in a disorganized mess.

Do have storage containers for other business, letting her materials sit ready and waiting right in front.

Don't think putting clutter behind your desk will get it out of the way.

Do remember that she'll be looking right at it when she's looking at you.

Don't reserve basic meeting supplies just for yourself.

Do have pens and a pad for her, too.

Don't go shuffling for necessary information or paperwork.

Do prepare in advance for whatever might come up.

4. Yourself

You don't have to look fancy, but you do have to look professional and put together. Your professionalism makes a woman feel more respected, more at ease. You want to look like someone she wants to talk to and wants to work with. No more, no less.

That means: Have a haircut. If you have a beard or mustache, keep it trimmed. Don't go to work with missing buttons, spots on your ties, or dryer wrinkles in your shirt, even if you figure they'll probably be hidden under a jacket. She'll notice them somehow.

In this game, it's not about the expense you go to, it's the effort you make. Today, "business casual" is everywhere—pants and a jacket rather than a suit and tie—but the trick is to know your customer. If she's conservative, kick your dress level up a notch; it might provide an advantage. If she's modern, a stylish touch might help you connect. When you can, lean toward the style of the client.

Whatever you wear, wear it well. Even an older suit can be freshened up with a new shirt or tie and polished shoes. When in doubt, do what it takes to dress well. If you're clueless about how to define this, consider a trip to a department store that offers personal shoppers. They can help you develop a style that works. For personal grooming, consider at least one visit to a higher-end barber shop or haircutter to get a good look for yourself—and learn how to maintain it easily.

Attention to Detail

Women notice the little things. They dig the details. You should, too. By doing so, you show you care about what she cares about. If you make the effort to sweat the smaller stuff, she'll feel valued.

Women notice the touches that bring a room together—a plant, a rug, a vase. These may seem to some like superficial niceties, but they have substantial value to many female customers. They can help create a warm environment that makes her feel secure and comfortable enough to move forward.

Bathrooms are a key area for women. I have a client who owns a large restaurant chain. When we recently surveyed customers about their dining experience, clean restrooms kept coming up as a consideration toward their patronage. Dirty bathrooms actually hurt sales. For men, bathrooms registered near zero on the significance scale.

Your restroom should always be clean, well lit (no burned-out bulbs), and kept up. "Empty" should be only for the garbage can—not the toilet tissue or soap dispenser. Women appreciate a mirror. Some other touches to consider: hand moisturizer and some potpourri to control odor.

You or someone else in your workplace should conduct a bathroom check every single day. It will be worth it.

Show Her Your Personal Side

Women want a connection whenever they do business. Women entrepreneurs think of their businesses like family; women consumers generally get their best product and service information from friends and colleagues; and all women prefer to buy from people who seem like they are on their side, looking out for them. If you put yourself out there as a person who cares about her, you'll set a tone of collaboration and personal connection that will inspire her to buy.

It doesn't take much—and the windfall could be big. Start by putting some kind of decoration on your desk or on an end table in the meeting area. It should be something that speaks; something that's yours. Park a plant or flowers there. Even a low-maintenance cactus will lend character to your workspace. It's always effective to display family photos or a picture of yourself with friends, because these bring you to life in her eyes.

And her eyes matter—literally. Women like a lot of eye contact. A study some years ago put groups of five-year-olds, half boys and half girls, in a room empty except for two chairs sitting side by side. At the end of five minutes, the boys were sitting or playing with the chairs just where they'd been at the start. The girls, on the other hand, long before that five minutes passed had moved the chairs so they faced each other. Females prefer to sit or play face to face so they can communicate. They trust people who look them in the eye. Here's a good guideline to follow: Give women at least 60 percent of the eye contact when selling to couples.

Some more rules you can count on: Shake hands first with the person closest to you, even if that's a woman and you are more comfortable starting with the man she may have walked in with. If you don't, she'll feel like a second-class citizen. (And she'll be right: First in, first shake—that's the standard.) Remember the "three foot rule"—sit or stand at about a three-foot distance from her. When standing up, it's more like 24 inches. If you're any closer, you're invading her space; farther, and you're too distant to connect. Again, this varies based on culture and comfort, so gauge your clients through nonverbal cues.

Make sure you hand her a card, and remind her that she can reach you anytime if she has a concern or question.

Use her name at least three times during the meeting. That way, you make sure you learn it, and you ensure she knows you really see her in two crucial respects: (1) as an individual, with distinct interests and needs as a customer; and (2) as a person worth knowing and remembering. You'll emphasize those essential messages if you use her name whenever appropriate. If you consult with a colleague at all during a meeting, always be sure to introduce your female customer by name.

Be a teammate, a real person on her side. Offer to put her briefcase with yours. Have a coffeemaker or water cooler, if feasible, and offer her something. If she accepts, have something with her while you talk.

In short, it's about making her feel comfortable working with you. You want to meet her in her comfort zone. That will facilitate the sale and go a long way toward building a lucrative relationship that lasts.

chapter six

Rethinking Victory

How You Close a Woman

In the end, it's all about the buy. Whatever else is involved in sales success, everybody in the business is looking for the right formula to close the sale. This is where women customers seem frustrating. No matter how much you've told them, they still have questions. They always want to think about it. They always want to discuss it with somebody else. Women always seem to throw up a roadblock or pull back from the brink just when you think you will get the yes.

It can drive a salesperson to avoid waiting on female customers as much as they can. What does it take to get her to take the plunge? A lot less than you might think. You need an adjusted outlook on your destination. The close looks different for women, and that means some new routes and routines are involved.

Once you can see where you're going and where the major pitfalls are, anybody can get there—again and again.

Wrong Turns: Directions To Avoid

Don't try this at home:

Sara: "Bob, I truly appreciate all this information, but I'd like time to go home and think about it."

Bob: "Don't think too long because I can't guarantee this rate after today. Why don't you go ahead and sign on, and if you decide later to cancel we can always reimburse your money within 48 hours."

Sara: "Thank you for the offer, but it's too large an investment for me to be hasty. As I said, let me think about it and I'll give you a call."

Bob: "I'll go one better: Let me secure your order today, and I'll reduce the initial investment by 10 percent. Would that help? Just tell me what it's going to take to get you to sign today."

Sara: "Again, your offer is attractive, but I've got to go. I'll call you when I make a decision."

What went wrong? Bob used high-pressure tactics that focused on impersonal incentives, such as time and money. "This is a great deal, why wait?" and "If you buy now, I'll give you a discount," are classic sales strategies that may work very well with men, but they don't tend to move women where you want them—and they may even chase women away.

What works better is a low-pressure sales approach. Women are particularly sensitive to feeling pushed or threatened, especially by men. If you think about it, you can probably imagine why. So, always keep her comfort level in mind. Watch for signs in her expression or body language that you are pushing too hard.

Some telltale signs of trouble that can be noted in her body language include: she seems to be withdrawing from you; she's anxious to end the conversation; she's making excuses to leave; her lips are clenched tight; she's frowning. You want the conversation to be comfortable moving forward—on both sides. If she seems cold or ill at ease, you're probably turning her off.

Beyond that, remember this: Price incentives are fine—who wouldn't like a discount?—but women are much more concerned about *value.* They are more likely to buy when you show them that the value of your product or service outweighs the cost, whatever it is.

But there is a rub: *Value must be linked to her needs and wants—not yours and not anybody else's.* It has to be all about the benefits specifically to her, in her expressed situation. Don't give her a general spiel about what the product or service offers; don't rest your case on how widely it's used. That's fine to include, but it's not targeted enough and it won't close the deal. Rather, you've got to show her how much the product or service offers *specifically for her needs* before she'll sign on the dotted line.

That's why I can't emphasize enough that listening is so important with women. If you can't apply your value proposition to her particular situation, she's much less likely to buy.

The good news, however, is your effort in listening will pay off—where it counts. Not only will listening let you know how to pitch product value, but it also will help you establish an amenable pace for the selling process. With female customers, it's about patience rather than persistence. Remember, women talk more than men do, and their talk is often a form of thinking out loud. They appreciate the time it takes to hear them out, and often reward it with the buy.

Be careful not to take her longer timeline as an invitation to wear her down until she gives in. That almost always backfires with women. Rather than relent, she is likely to shut down, build a wall around herself, or retreat—none of which will help you close the sale.

A slower pace may be challenging to maintain, but don't resort to game playing to push her into closing. Men are more competitive than women in the sales process. They enjoy jousting and the adversarial challenge that culminates in a sense of triumph at the close. Women typically don't do combat, and they don't see the appeal in a sales process that has silently become concerned with one side dominating or overtaking the other.

It follows then that too much banter or too many clever attempts to lure her into the deal won't go over well either. Women are particularly sensitive to feeling they're being maneuvered. Don't roll your pen across the table and tell her with a wink she can keep it if she signs. Don't try shallow compliments to butter her up for the buy. Women want salespeople to show them the value then let them make their own choices, while remaining right by their side to help them do it well.

That's what brings you the buy. The big bottom line: *Women prefer buying by cooperating. They like to feel they're on the same team with their salespeople, that the two of you are working together toward a shared goal.* As a result, they are more likely to buy when the dynamic is collaborative. To close a woman, you must show her the value and set up the process so you and she are full partners in a win-win.

"I Need To Think About It"

When a woman says, "I need to think about it," it's not just a sneaky way of saying, "No thanks, I'm leaving." When she asks another question or wants to consult someone else, it's not a backhanded insult to your knowledge or integrity. Yet many salespeople get defensive or annoyed in these situations—and sometimes a little angry.

When a woman customer signals she isn't ready to buy, however, she's actually telling you something useful: She hasn't gotten enough information yet. Think of her question as a sign of interest—and use it as a guide to where you go from there.

Here are some tactics to try:

1. Emphasize Points of Agreement

Go ahead and try this at home:

Sara: "Bob, I truly appreciate all this information, but I'd like to go home and think about it."

Bob: "I understand; it's important to feel comfortable with this investment. Before you leave, I'd like to go over a few points you

should make note of when reviewing the mate-
rial. Please keep in mind, Sara, that our product
meets all the criteria you felt were important,
such as service requirements, date of delivery,
and payment terms. Most important is that we
provide the best service for your needs and will
guarantee service within 24 hours so there will
be minimal downtime for your company."

You don't necessarily need to come up with something new, and you definitely don't need to do a full-
court press at the end. Rather, lock in points you
know are winners with her. Remind her how much
she has liked what you've already had to say.

Remember to keep it personal—use her name,
mention her company or industry, keep her specific
needs front and center to the end. Try using personal
analogies, which emphasize the points and continue
to build the teamwork connection between you. You
could offer an analogy to when you or a friend or a
relative was making an important purchasing decision similar to the one above, where getting everything you want and need at a fair price was what

mattered—not getting the lowest price no matter what.

2. Accept Responsibility

A client or customer has the right to object. It's crucial to recognize that right, so resist the impulse to correct or fix her. Don't rebut or challenge her objection, even if you think it is invalid or incorrect. Instead, acknowledge that you understand her concern and treat it as a misunderstanding. Accept responsibility for it and ask for her help in getting back on track:

> **Steven:** "Jane, I understand your concerns, but I am confident that we provide the best product and service to meet your needs. And because our pricing is competitive, I must take responsibility for having not conveyed the value well. I would appreciate it if you would share where I went off course."

Most people, but especially women, tend to react to this kind of response in a supportive way. She'll want to help you better understand what's holding her back. Before you know it, you'll have her on your side and you'll hear what her true challenges are so you can address them.

> ***Jane:*** "No, Steven, you did a fine job relating the value of your service. Actually, we had a recent budget cut and what I thought I could afford at the time is no longer an option."
>
> ***Steven:*** "Jane, I may have a solution for you, or at least an option to think about. We have a product that is comparable, but it has fewer features—features that would not be critical to your operation. It would allow you to comfortably upgrade with the same service benefits."
>
> ***Jane:*** "Sounds interesting. Tell me more . . ."

3. Reframe the Value—In Her Terms

To get a woman to move forward, you might need to do more than meet her specific purchasing criteria. Remember, with women, the buy is bigger than those specifics. It's about benefits, widely defined. She thinks in contexts. She thinks in relationships. She thinks with her feelings, too, blending her heart with her head. It's a different perspective, a different value system. For these reasons, you'll need to communicate value points to close her.

For instance, a woman may come in to buy a car saying she'll pay at most $400 a month for a loan. That's her price. If you sell her enough on broader benefits, though, she might recalculate. If you point to safety benefits, security benefits, service benefits, maintenance support, transport to and from the office should the car need service—any and all of these are benefits beyond the specs that might sell the car, maybe even at a higher price. Suddenly, she might place the value for this purchase closer to $500 a month—or more.

She'll come up with additional money beyond what she's budgeted because the car now seems worth more. You've given it greater value to her.

Essentially, you have reframed the sale. You have changed the frame of reference from price per month to value in her life. You have put it into a new perspective, and one that's more likely to resonate for her. Can you offer her service beyond what's she's used to? Can you show long-term benefits that specifically relate to her situation? These are the kinds of value points that make a product worth having to a woman—and even worth paying more for.

Another way to reframe involves quality. Can you talk beyond her needs to her wants? Can you help her fulfill an indulgence? A client of mine related the following experience she had in shopping in a department store for a new suit. She wanted to spend about $300. When approached by a sales associate, she quickly shared her budget requirements and was directed to a specific area to meet her price range. She didn't find what she wanted, so she left and went to a neighboring store.

There she was similarly greeted by a sales associate, who was given the same budget considerations. This associate went further, exploring the particulars of what my client was seeking. It turned out that a more expensive designer offered a suit that met all her requests except that it was higher in price. The salesperson encouraged her to try it on and experience the quality and exceptional comfort. She also went on to explain that the life of the suit would be considerably longer and combined all the features to justify the investment. My client said she was sold—

and frequently shops with the same sales associate, who has earned her trust.

Similar logic can sell appliances or computer peripherals or cars or homes. It demands only that you take the time and make the effort to frame the value of an item—in her terms.

4. Share Relationships

Does the following sound familiar?

Brenda: "That's great, Ron. Just give me some time to review the contract and I'll be back in touch."

Ron: "Brenda, I recognize that this investment is a substantial one for you, so I want to make sure you're comfortable with the purchase. I am confident this product will meet and most likely exceed your needs. Hey, I work with another woman business owner who bought this product, and I've heard several times from her about how delighted she is with it. I'm happy to connect the two of you or give you her number—she said she's happy to be called as a referral."

Brenda: "That's very nice of you, Ron. Tell me more about her business and how she used the product advantageously."

Ron: "She networked her business so the product cut down on the amount of . . . So, as you can see, not only has it proven highly reliable, it also cut her cost enough to offset the investment. Pretty soon, she told me, it will provide positive cash flow."

Brenda: "Sounds intriguing. Okay, Ron, let's go over the payment terms and initial deposit one more time . . ."

What made this pitch work? There were three key points of connection. First, Ron showed Brenda that he had other female customers like her. He has experience working with women, and is successful working with them. Next, he showed her he remembered them, and knew their businesses in some detail. This demonstrates that he really listens and cares about his customers' needs. Last, he knew why the product works well for his customers. This shows he's dependable and follows up.

5. A Dose of Urgency—In the Context of Consideration

Still need to get her off the fence? Try a dose of urgency—but in the context of consideration. It's crucial to keep her needs, and her interests, front and center if you want to close the deal.

Think about the following:

- "Karen, you shared how important it was for you to have your home ready for the holidays. I don't want to disappoint you. I promise you'll have delivery of the furniture in time for the holidays, if you place the order today."

- "Joyce, I know financial decisions need serious reflection, but being able to do year-end adjustments could save you X amount in tax time, so moving forward sooner rather than later might be the smartest thing to do. Keep in mind, I'll be with you throughout this process."

- "Daniella, a home is a big commitment, but moving forward quickly is the only way to be sure you can be settled in before your kids start the new school year. I'm confident that this investment is exactly what you're looking for."

These kinds of statements, packaged with a touch of emotion, reassurance, and connection, can make her see that buying now is what's best for her.

You Don't Close a Woman; You Come To an Agreement

The point that you need to clearly understand is: When selling to women, you don't close. While this may sound nuts, it's true. You don't close a woman; you come to an agreement.

When doing business with female customers or clients, it is essential to wrap your head around this conceptual difference: Selling is not a competition or a game, it's a relationship. Thus, closing is not a triumph for you and a kind of defeat for the customer; it's a win-win. With women, the concept is teamwork. You join forces to conclude what product or service is in her best interest. You come together to give her the best value she can get. And you make it clear that you plan to be there, on her team, beyond the single deal or sale today.

To close in this context, most of all you've got to have her trust. This doesn't just happen. It comes through a series of steps. It is developed—beginning with how you introduce yourself the minute she walks in the door and continuing through the way you maintain the relationship after she signs on the dotted line.

There are several background factors that contribute to her trust—such as the perceived value of the company you work for and the company's reputation—but there's only so much you can do about these if they don't tip the scales your way. Don't deny bad company press if she brings it up, but turn as quickly as you can to the trust factors you *can* control.

If you are an independent sales agent or part of a franchise, your local business has a reputation of its own. What are you doing within your community to support local causes, schools, or charities? Are you known in your community? Do you sit on boards or committees? Do you sponsor local events? It's important to build your own reputation.

Additional building blocks for building trust include:

- Start off on the right foot by offering a warm, respectful greeting. Learn her name. Remember, the buy-in begins with "hello."

- Next comes the listening phase. Pay attention. Just listen. (See active listening skills in Chapter 3.)

- Now comes the benefits stage. Talk about the value points of the product or service for her particular situation.

- Then listen some more. This can give you decisive information and also develops rapport. (For tips on addressing her responses, see Chapter 5.)

- As you approach the close—to her, an agreement—follow steps 1 through 4 from earlier in this chapter.

chapter seven

Winning For Keeps

The Added Value of Brand-loyal Women

OK, you've shown her the value. You've shared your success stories, and you've nudged her with a dose of urgency. Finally, you've closed the deal. Finished. Over and out.

Well, not exactly. You could stop there—take your sale to the bank and call it a good day—but if you did, you'd be cheating yourself out of a wave of even better days ahead. To ride that baby, you'll need to continue the relationship beyond the close. The truth is, with women customers, closing is just the beginning—but it can be the beginning of a beautiful thing.

If you're wondering why you should continue the relationship after an exhaustive courtship, the answer is quite simple: Because a satisfied female customer is more likely to come back with repeat business. You see, women like relationships. They like to be in relationships, even with salespeople. That's where they live—and buy.

Remember: *Women are twice as likely as male customers to make referrals.* When you create and sustain a relationship with a female customer, you set up a system that will pay off in multiples down the road. They'll stick with you, and they'll build your pipeline of referrals by spreading the word. That adds up to consistent future income.

Just do the math: Long-term loyalty plus customer-generating referrals equals a major multiplication of your business. If you put in the extra time now, your sales curve will head upward as far as the eye can see. You can take that to the bank.

Making the Relationship Last

Building the relationship beyond the close takes a little bit of time and a little bit of thought—but it can pay big dividends for a long time to come. All it really takes is some attention to a very simple idea: Keep in touch. Women like follow-up. That's what a relationship is all about—staying in contact over time. Women want to know that you are there for them and that they can count on you. This begins the minute you close the sale, and should continue as long as you want to keep her as a customer (and her network of referrals, too).

This might sound like a lot to deal with, but in fact, there are a few simple things you should do to make the relationship last after the close. Here's a step-by-step guide.

1. Send a Thank-you Note

While thank-you notes may seem like a nicety from a bygone era, you'd be surprised how much this simple gesture still resonates with women customers. It doesn't have to be elaborate, just a sentence or two to let her know you appreciate her business. A smart card will also provide a friendly reminder that you're available for her future needs. Here is a short sample, with wording that won't steer you wrong:

Dear Loretta,

Thank you for the opportunity to provide our services. I am confident that our products and exceptional service department will exceed your expectations. I am devoted to the satisfaction of my clients, so please do not hesitate to contact me should you have any questions or concerns.

I also appreciate your referral should you know of anyone who would benefit from our services.

Again, thank you. I will be in touch on a periodic basis, just to check in.

Sincerely,

Rick Salesperson

2. Check In

Personally contact her to see if she's happy with the product or service. You don't have to open a whole can of worms with this. You don't have to ask her point blank, "Are there any problems?" All you want to do is let her know you care how she's doing since the sale. Should a problem or need arise during the conversation, though, pledge to help and follow through. Do not disappoint her.

3. Be a Strategic Partner

When an article, report, or some piece of information crosses your path that might be of interest or use to her, send it along. This reminds her that you are a strategic partner, on her team for good. If it's electronic, just forward it to her e-mail; if it's paper, attach a sticky note with a simple sentence saying you thought this might be of interest. Don't just write *FYI*. Compose at least one complete sentence expressing why you thought this might be helpful, that you care about her needs, that you want to help her business grow, or whatever the case may be.

4. Remember Her Anniversary

Make a note in your calendar so you can touch base with her on selected occasions. This will personalize the relationship and give you another chance to remind her of your products or services. Send a holiday card for sure. If you know her birthday, send a card, or, if possible, offer a small token (a glass of wine at a local restaurant, a carnation or tulip from a local florist) to acknowledge it. My favorite high-impact forget-me-not: Send a card or e-mail marking the anniversary of your business relationship.

5. Go the Extra Mile

When appropriate, send referrals for related products or services that might be valuable to her. Everyone appreciates new business, and the fact that you keep them in mind will go a long way in maintaining a trusted and valuable relationship. Just be careful here; you don't want her to think you are more interested in helping your friends get new business than in helping her.

6. See Her Again

When you have new products or services, schedule a follow-up meeting. Let her know that you have something new that you want to bring her in on. Let her know that the new product is a continuation or an enhancement of your business relationship by suggesting some ways it might link to the needs or issues or ideas she has previously shared with you. Even if you don't have product updates, make a point of reconnecting, just to keep the relationship current.

To make this stick, you've got to be the kind of salesperson she trusts. Essentially, that means be there—correct service problems immediately, and always return customer calls within 24 hours. (If you can't do it yourself, make sure someone else does. Always.)

Riding the Extra Mile

Maintaining the trust of a female customer is not as time-consuming as building it, but it still takes some effort. Women tend to be less trusting than men, perhaps especially with male salespeople. Chalk it up to a few bad apples that spoil the reputation of the bunch. Trust is the bedrock of your relationship with a woman customer, and it always will be.

If you want to maintain her trust, you will have to let her talk. You will have to avoid sounding cocky or slick, pushy or arrogant. You will need to recommend, not command. You will need to listen, listen, and listen some more. For as long as you do business together, you will always need to deal with her on the same terms.

This will get easier and easier over time. By the time you close, you will know her better. You'll know her business, her family, her emotional triggers, and her style. As a result, you won't have to listen less, but you'll probably be in a position to listen less long. Sales discussions will become simpler, and they might even get more direct. People acquainted with each other develop a shorthand when they talk. That not only affirms the trust between you, but also cuts out some of the filler you find in first-time conversations.

Over time, you'll become more adept at cross-gender selling. You might always prefer a customer of your own gender; you might not. In any case, you'll become more ambidextrous, more of a switch hitter, so the adjustments you make will feel more natural. That comfort, in turn, will help you present with greater sincerity. With that, you'll build trust with others and deepen the trust of those whose business you've already won.

(chapter eight)

Putting It Into Play

Notes Before You Go

I train thousands of sales professionals a year, and over and over I have heard them share experiences with women. In particular, financial advisors claim that it takes anywhere from six to eight conversations to close a woman versus two to three to close the deal with a man. This sure makes it sound like men are the low-hanging fruit! They are easier to close and, therefore, you can close more of them, right? This sounds like a solid business rationale for avoiding women customers.

What I've found to be true, however, is that this kind of thinking is shortsighted, and provides less of a basis for long-term success. You see, while men take fewer steps to purchase, they are also less inclined to customer loyalty and are less likely to refer your product or service than are women. Looking at the big picture, the real formula for success goes something like this: *The time spent acquiring and retaining women customers will ultimately lead to more business generated per customer, twice as many referrals, and a tendency to create greater word-of-mouth marketing for you and your brand.* So while the low-hanging fruit may seem attractive, it's actually the more challenging pickings that will fill your coffers long term. Women are worth the extra effort!

So what does the extra effort look like? Here are some final notes on putting it all into play.

Not all sales experiences are alike. Some have longer sales cycles, some have shorter ones. You wouldn't think you'd sell financial services or homes the same way you'd sell appliances or apparel. In terms of pacing, you'd be right. In terms of content, you'd be wrong—and it would be a costly mistake.

Actually, short-cycle selling goes against the grain of how women buy. For women, buying tends to be more of an emotional process, and they frequently take more time in decision-making than men do. Women have a greater tendency than men to walk away to give the purchase more thought. This may happen regardless of how good you are. She may need more time, but, rest assured, if she had a great sales experience, she will return.

Long or short cycle, that great sales experience means touching on every stage of the selling to women process you've learned in this book. Every stage is an important step in building her trust. Remember, to her, she's entering a relationship, not just buying a stove. In products with shorter sales cycles, you've got to move through the steps faster, but you've got to move through all of them just the same. To that extent, there is no difference between selling stocks or selling shoes to women.

Following Figure 8.1 (on page 118) is a breakdown of each stage, with some final notes you'll need to put it all together and win.

figure 8.1   Snapshot: The Seven Steps to Selling to Women

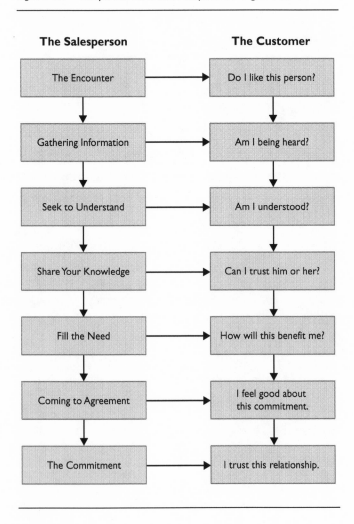

The Salesperson	The Customer
The Encounter	Do I like this person?
Gathering Information	Am I being heard?
Seek to Understand	Am I understood?
Share Your Knowledge	Can I trust him or her?
Fill the Need	How will this benefit me?
Coming to Agreement	I feel good about this commitment.
The Commitment	I trust this relationship.

Step 1: The Encounter

Goal: To start off winning.

It is during this initial encounter that a woman customer will determine if she likes you enough to continue. People like to do business with people they
like. The encounter stage is all about making her
comfortable and establishing rapport. With women,
this is more important than it might seem. In fact,
how you handle the introduction and breaking the
ice will determine if she feels comfortable enough to
move forward to the next step. If you don't create
the right first encounter, you will have a difficult time
making up for it through the process; you will have
reduced your chances of converting her to a customer before you've barely begun.

Some say a first impression is formed in less than
one minute. Remember that the sale begins even
before you say hello. It begins when she enters your
office building or as she opens the door and meets
you for the first time.

So take a minute to take an imaginary walk in her
shoes. What immediate experience does she have?

Are your surroundings inviting? Is she greeted by a friendly receptionist? Does your office or waiting room impart credibility, reliability, and trustworthiness—or do you need to revamp?

What if you are meeting her for the first time outside of your office? Then your physical being is her first encounter with your organization, so there's a heavier burden on you personally to be well dressed and groomed. Don't forget, women will assume that the way you conduct yourself away from your office reflects how you behave in your work. Being on time speaks volumes to most people about whether they can trust you in business.

Now greet her. Don't forget that a clear sign of respect is that you shake the hand of the person standing closest to you first and then proceed to shake hands with any others. Remember to shake her hand firmly but not hard, simply firm enough to denote respect and that you are truly pleased to meet her. Give everyone—including her and anyone else who might be accompanying her—your card.

Of course, it's assumed that you recognize the importance of appearance and manners. A smile, a sincere handshake, looking her in the eye as you are speaking—all need to take place.

To help you better understand what it takes to truly resonate with women, answer these questions honestly. If you can answer yes to all, then you are off to a good start:

- Are you likeable?
- Do you make a good first impression?
- Do you come across as warm and genuine?
- Do you smile enough?
- Do you know the protocol when meeting women prospects?
- Do you typically break the ice by finding common ground?

So now the sales process you recognize begins. Remember that for women especially, trust results in sales, and the sooner she trusts you, the sooner you will close the sale and move forward with a viable long-term relationship. According to research, association counts when it comes to women. They appreciate being on common ground. Family and community associations are great conversation starters—that's one big reason why it's important to keep signs of family and community involvement in your office. Simple comments, such as *"I hear you have a 12-year-old son, my daughter is just turning 13. Great and challenging years ahead I'm led to believe,"* can help you get to common ground. One financial producer shared that he likes injecting humor into common areas of interest. Women do enjoy good humor—who doesn't?—and it quickly puts you on the same wavelength.

Getting off on the right foot is the foundation for success, whether your sales process happens in minutes or months. How you initially break the ice and make a connection will mean the difference in your pocket. Let's assume that you are a car salesperson. When a woman walks into your showroom, do you give her a chance to browse first or do you approach her upon her arrival and introduce yourself? Most of the time, women will appreciate having a salesperson approach them fairly quickly because they tend not to be as comfortable in the dealership sales process. This is your chance to put her at ease and begin the introduction process that will make her recognize from the start that you are the salesperson she wants to work with.

Here's an example of how you can approach her.

Welcome. Thank you for visiting our show-room. My name is John Pederson and I would be delighted to answer any questions or just discuss our products. May I ask your name?

Of course, we're making the assumption that you recognize the importance of appearance and mannerisms. A smile, a sincere handshake, looking her in the eye as you are speaking, handing her your card during the introduction, should have all taken place. Next is to use her name as you begin to ask her questions. Making her comfortable and at ease with you as a person is critical so you can move to the next step—seeking information.

Checklist

What you know you need to do:

- ❑ Make a good first impression (appearance).
- ❑ Be on time.
- ❑ Maintain eye contact.
- ❑ Offer your card.
- ❑ Remember to smile.

❏ Be aware of your environment.

❏ Use ice breakers.

Step 2: Gathering Information

Goal: To capture the information necessary to position your product in her terms.

The information-gathering stage sounds misleadingly simple. In actuality, it's the most critical phase in the selling to women process. And it isn't easy. With women, you must do more than listen closely and gather relevant facts—which, due to communication differences, may be difficult enough for some. You must be exceptional at capturing the kind of information necessary to situate your product or services as a solution to her needs, in her terms. You need to figure out and use the kind of information necessary to position your product or services in her life, goals, and dreams.

This is probably the most critical step of them all; it's also the step salespeople are most likely to rush through or skip over entirely with women. Selling effectively to a woman means getting to know her—asking what she does, how she does it, where she does it, when she does it, who she does it with, and why she does it that way. Only then are you equipped with the information to ask how you can help her do it better.

Whether her lifestyle or what she does has anything to do with the product or services you are selling is irrelevant, but getting to know her is. Let's face it: How do we know what we're recommending will make sense to the other person? Well, we don't, unless we've gathered the right information and can apply it so that it makes sense to her and her lifestyle. That is why this step is the most critical step of the sales process.

We spent a lot of time on listening skills in Chapter 3, but especially with women this is typically where you will win her over or lose her sale. As a reminder, when asking questions, try to always ask open-ended questions, the ones that begin with who, what, where, when, and how.

The information-gathering step will have more impact only if you are successful in Step 1, in establishing a comfortable rapport. Ask yourself: Would you open up more to someone you take a liking to than to someone who you don't connect with? Of course, we are all human and all of us gravitate to people we like. It's here in Step 2 where she will determine if you "get it," and, more importantly, if you "get her"—what she wants, needs, and prefers. Your listening skills will allow you the insight into what she truly wants versus what she needs.

Because you have successfully made it through Step 1, she may be delighted that you seem to "get it." Those initial feelings of trust will work in your favor now in helping you gain access to critical insights that will win a woman's business.

Checklist

What you know you need to do:

- ❑ Remember the listening rules.
- ❑ Take notes.
- ❑ Identify needs, issues, preferences, and categories of interest.
- ❑ Give her your full attention.

Step 3: Seek To Understand

Goal: To demonstrate to her that she was heard and understood.

Here is where you will summarize the information you gathered to clarify the facts and demonstrate your understanding of her unique needs. Showing that you understand her is critical because women will buy from you not because they understand what you're selling but because you understand how and what they are buying. Let me repeat: *Many women will buy from you not because they understand what you are selling but because you understand them!*

You've asked all the right questions and now your job is to translate this information back to her so that she is confident that you truly heard her and understand her. Reinforcing the information will take the form of a summary of key points that you will use to support the product or service benefits. If this is a same-day sale, reviewing her needs and preferences will be done verbally. If your sale takes place in multiple meetings, then a follow-up letter is appropriate to further cement your understanding. In this case, the letter should be mailed within 48 hours. Snail mail please, unless she is traveling and then an e-mail would be appropriate. In that letter you should reconfirm three or more points of interest. Share with her how pleased you are to have spent time with her and that you are eager and committed to supporting her goals. The letter should be positive and appreciative, and it should contain bullet points of interest that will be discussed in detail during your next meeting. Share with her multiple ways in which she can reach you should she have any additional questions. A follow-up letter allows her the opportunity to reflect on what was discussed and to provide additional feedback or clarification. This process can spare you time, money, and frustration because many people tend to change their mind as to purchasing requirements.

In addition, you may want to follow up with a call, especially if you have to answer additional questions in order to complete the proposal. A call can be anything from simply confirming that she received your letter to asking a few more questions. End the call on the note that you are looking forward to your next meeting and to call you should she have any questions in the meantime.

Checklist

What you know you need to do:

- ❑ Translate back findings.
- ❑ Clarify needs assessment.
- ❑ Review key preferences.
- ❑ Reaffirm eagerness to meet her needs.
- ❑ Offer to give more information, if needed.

Step 4: Share Your Knowledge

Goal: To empower her with insight and information.

When sharing your knowledge, confidence shows. Women appreciate a salesperson who is knowledge-able and secure—but not arrogant. The difference is your confidence should result from having in-depth knowledge and mastery—both of your products or services and her needs and concerns. Women appreciate a salesperson who is competent and confident, but never a know-it-all. You need to present the sale in a professional and informative format that allows her to feel comfortable with your product knowledge.

Remember, to her, the sales process is not a competition; it's a relationship. Confidence means admitting when you don't know the answer to her question, and then getting the answer to her within 24 hours.

To a woman, confidence becomes arrogance when it is unearned, unjustified, and/or used to push or bully her into making a purchase that serves your interests instead of hers.

So how do you provide the best sales experience during this phase? Think "Give."

A woman will buy when she feels confident about her decision. What women want is information enabling them to gain the confidence they need to move the sale forward. What they want is the knowledge necessary to make a good decision for themselves.

Here's an example. I phoned my financial advisor to discuss a college fund savings program that seemed to have strong advantages. He immediately responded that the program is not appropriate for us, and shared his recommendations as to the program he considered more suitable to our needs. I thanked him and got off the phone. I ended the call frustrated. Why? He bulldozed me with an answer without letting me finish explaining the issue and didn't bother to give me the information or reasoning that led up to it. Basically, he presumed to mind read, then told me what to do. He didn't listen or provide me with the information I needed to decide what would be best for me.

Even if you think you know what a woman customer or client should buy, she will likely find it arrogant and insulting if you just tell her what it is. The decision must be hers. To her, a salesperson should advise—not tell. Here's an alternative scenario that would have sealed the deal.

> *Me:* "Hi, Art. I heard about a college fund product that I'd like to consider purchasing for our girls."
>
> *Art:* "Terrific Delia, let me share with you how that program works and then we can discuss if it's the right fit with your portfolio."

After ten minutes of sharing information on the program, Art will then ask if I understand the advantages and disadvantages. He will then proceed to recommend a similar product that would support our college saving goals as well as provide us additional advantages more in line with our portfolio. By taking the time to provide me with the information I need to feel confident about my decision, Art is enabling me to move forward with his recommendations.

When selling to women, play a supportive role during this step. Provide the information that is essential to moving closer to the close. Let her take the lead. Don't forget: Women don't need—and don't want—you to "fix it." Let me emphasize that if information is *not* presented supportively and respectfully, many women will walk away—with a bad impression of you top of mind and on the tip of their tongues.

I can illustrate this with another true story. I recently went to the mall with my daughters and we decided to buy a hair dryer that would be powerful enough to dry our thick hair faster. The owner of a hair care store spent over 30 minutes sharing with us his knowledge (former hair stylist) on the different textures of our hair and the products that would enhance them. Interestingly, I never truly noticed that while all of us had thick hair, my youngest had much finer hair than mine, and my other daughter had an in-between texture that was quite different than either of ours.

The owner took the time to explain how to best manage and maintain each of ours individually, and showed us different products we could use to enhance our hair. He gave us samples to take home and test. When we finally got to the hair dryers, he explained that if we wanted to do what was best for our hair, we each needed a different type of dryer. As you may have already guessed, we ended up with three dryers! We spent substantially more than we had in mind, but once we were educated consumers, we were able to justify the additional costs relative to how our new products were going to enhance the health and look of our hair. We could see the value, even in spending more.

The owner was an excellent salesman in that he understood that the best way to sell to women is to teach them what they need to know to buy what's best. Again, the cost exceeded what I had had in mind, but the value he helped me understand allowed me to comfortably make the additional purchases. In addition, while I found his store more expensive, we all agreed we would return.

If you do present information right, you may achieve a level of trust that will lead to what appear to be buying signs, but be advised: A common mistake with women is misreading comfort with buying signs. A second mistake—much harder to repair—is then allowing perceived buying signs to trigger hard-sell techniques. Be careful not to make either mistake, but if you make the first, you can keep your sale on track by not making the second. As a rule, women don't respond well to the hard sell, especially in cross-gender situations.

Here are a few "back off" warning signs:

- She starts to find excuses why she needs to leave.
- She says she needs to think about it so that she can leave.
- She backs away physically.
- She starts looking at her watch.
- Her face becomes tense or tight.
- She is easily distracted.

If you notice these signals, immediately turn the conversation around so that you are focusing on what she needs to hear, not what you want her to do.

What you are going for is deepening buy-in throughout the sales process.

When we are selling we sometimes get caught up in getting: getting the commitment, getting the signature, getting the commission. A good salesperson will know when the time is right to ask for the business, especially with women. So let her give you the buying signals, and in the meantime focus not on getting, but on giving. Give her materials, books, resources—whatever you have that is appropriate based on her interests. Remember, women tend to do more research than men, then tend to comparison shop and compare notes more, so provide her with materials before the encounter ends. If you want to customize the information, then assure her that you will have the specified information to her within days—and be sure you do.

Checklist

What you know you need to do:

- ❑ Empower her with information.
- ❑ Get her buy-in throughout the presentation.
- ❑ Give her materials to further her knowledge.

Step 5: Fill the Need

Goal: To position your product or service as a solution to her need.

While each step gets you closer to closing the deal, it is this interim step that will get her buy-in so that she can come to an agreement. It's your job to have identified her needs, preferences, challenges, and experiences earlier in the process, and then throughout the course of the sale, to reinforce how your product or services will fill the need. And not just any need. *Her* unique or particular need. It is here that you will present evidence of the effectiveness of your product or service by clearly showing how it will become the solution she has been seeking. Understand that her most pressing question is: "What will it do for me?" To effectively sell to women, you must answer this question to their complete satisfaction.

Many people buy value more than they concern themselves with cost. Demonstrating value is a step in the right direction, but with women the decision will be a result of even more factors. To build the odds in your favor it's best to reinforce your level of commitment to her, your level of confidence in the product or services to fill her needs, and then, of course, support this with the value proposition. For example, in financial services, women want a "partner" in providing solutions more than they want a salesperson. Her needs today may be quite different than her needs in ten years, so she will be selecting an advisor who she can establish a long-term relationship with, because she will be confident that this person will be proactive in identifying her changing needs and provide solutions throughout the course of their relationship.

In general, a salesperson can capitalize on establishing himself as the one who appreciates the changing needs of his customers and is eager to provide better solutions over time. Remember: Women prefer ongoing relationships; they like to buy from someone who understands them, their needs, preferences, and buying style, and from salespeople who will work with them to find the best solution.

Checklist

What you know you need to do:

- ❏ Connect benefits to needs.
- ❏ Provide value that exceeds cost.
- ❏ Be the solution.

Step 6: Coming To an Agreement

Goal: To make her feel good about this commitment.

Asking for a commitment from her takes nothing more or less than reassuring her that your "agreement" will meet her needs. Reminding her of the points discussed and reiterating how the product or services will meet those needs, will provide you with the opportunity to move forward. *"I am certain that this is the best product and service for you. I just want to make sure you are happy with everything we've covered. Is there anything further you need to go over or shall we move forward?"* Or simply, *"Shall we move forward?"* should make it clear this is the time to decide and buy. Women will appreciate the idea of the "we" versus "you" because it reinforces that you are a team.

Let's assume you are doing everything right and you still get the dreaded "I need to think about it" response. Don't sweat it. Remember that when a woman says *I need to think about it,* she may well mean just that. She may do a bit more research, seek input from others, or just want to give the decision additional thought, but rest assured that she is keeping her word. Your best move is probably to just go with her, offering to provide whatever information is practical for her further review.

There may, however, be a short cut. You may be able to stay a step ahead by providing referrals of other women or clients who have benefited from the same service. This could quench her need to collaborate with others who you don't know and can't talk to. Try something like this:

> Mary, I would love to introduce you to another client of mine that had a very similar situation. She chose this investment program. It has enabled her to maintain the monthly income level she needs and given her enough

money left over to indulge in a vacation and frequent trips to visit her grandchildren. She has graciously offered herself as a referral.

If all the steps were followed correctly, there should be no reason why she would not move forward. Yet sometimes an additional issue will surface right when it's time to sign. Don't panic. Think of whatever she says is holding her back as a "response"—not an objection. If you hear it that way you can deal with it and move forward. With women, the issue is usually that she needs more information or affirmation before she proceeds. Below are some steps you can take:

- If she needs additional time to "think about it," be polite and caring and reinforce benefits. Should she continue to need more time, let her know that you will follow up with her soon. Being gently persistent with women works as well, but women are subtle communicators and respond to a salesperson who knows how to gauge their follow-ups.

- If you are truly unsure as to why she will not agree to move forward, then simply take responsibility for not having explained the benefits effectively enough and apologize. She will typically be quick to open a dialogue as to the true issue holding her back.

- If you are confident that what you offer is the very best solution, then be patient. Respectfully ask her to review why your product or service is the best solution, and assure her that you will be available when she is ready to move forward.

- Most important: Be sincere about your interest in helping her make the right decision for her!

Keep in mind that not all women are alike. For a no-nonsense business owner, a crystal clear presentation of benefits and value might make the difference— especially if it is finely tuned to her needs. In a recent survey conducted by *MedeliaMonitor: The Voice of Women in America,* we found that a high priority for women is a clear presentation that succinctly demonstrates how the product or service will address her needs. When businesswomen hold off, seeking outside opinions, it is often because clarity isn't there. Many women may need to spend more time gathering consensus from others before making a decision. This is where providing referrals can provide assurance and move the decision-making process ahead. Another type of woman may be eager to please and would want to move forward faster than expected. While this is a pleasant trait to any salesperson, play it safe by reviewing all benefits and service features, because it's critical that the customer does not regret the purchasing decision later on.

Checklist

What you know you need to do:

- ❏ Reassure and reinforce benefits as solutions.
- ❏ Reinforce that your relationship will not end with the sale.
- ❏ Use referrals to close confidence holes.
- ❏ Ask permission to move forward.

Step 7: The Commitment

Goal: To get her to trust the relationship.

Women place more value on relationships than men do when it comes to the buying process. Once you come to an agreement and cement the sale, you can now begin to demonstrate your unique selling style. That is, now you show her you genuinely care about an ongoing relationship with her and the people in her life (because they will influence her decision making). She built trust along the way—trust enough to move forward with the sale—but the real test comes after she agrees. You have the responsibility to care for her account after the transaction as much as or more so than prior to the sale.

I find that women's purchasing decisions are more driven by emotional triggers than are men's. After they've emotionally committed to the buy, they justify their decision logically. That means they need to take that decision "halo effect" and carry it through so there are no regrets.

What does that mean for you? Follow through. It's imperative with women that you do not betray their trust. If you say you are going to do something, do it. If you are away or delayed or otherwise unable to follow up as promised, make sure someone else in your organization does it for you. Regardless, always call to check in and make sure all went as promised, especially if you delegated the task to others.

It's the salesperson who is ultimately responsible for customer satisfaction. Be the keeper of the relationship and follow up as much as necessary to reassure your commitment to her account. A female customer is worth her weight in gold, so treat her accordingly. Remember, she is a natural word-of-mouth marketer and will reward your commitment by praising you to everyone she knows, or, in contrast, she will tell everyone she sees that you have disappointed her and discourage others from doing business with you. Basically, you never want her to regret her decision to trust you. Ever.

Trust is a changing dynamic that can be easily upset if the customer's expectations are not met. Luckily, there are only a few bedrock basics involved in cementing a long-lasting and profitable relationship. Here's the deal:

- Carry through on all paperwork and deliverables.
- Tell the truth. Clear communication is key to managing expectations and preventing disappointments after the fact.
- Keep your word. Follow up with her to make sure all deliverables and promises are met to

her satisfaction. Most dissatisfied women customers complain that the salesperson did not meet their expectations following the sale.

■ Keep in touch. Remembering women customers throughout the year will have its rewards. Sending a card for the holidays, on her birthday, or on the anniversary of the sale, for example, will leave a lasting impression. Articles of interest or relevance, sent with a brief note, can have a big impact on her. Be more than a resource; be interested in her success. Never let her forget that you want to be on her team.

Checklist

What you know you need to do:

- ❑ Take your commitments to heart.
- ❑ Follow through on all commitments.
- ❑ Maintain and build your relationship.

(chapter nine)

Making the Leap

OK, we've reached the end of the playbook. The practice is done. It's time to play. You're prepped. You're ready. You now know exactly what you need to do to make the connection and build trust, to speak her language, to close her, to keep her coming back for more. Now the ball is in your court.

The very last move you need to make isn't physical. It's a leap you've got to take mentally. It's a mental switch. You've got to make it, take it seriously, and start seeing women in a new light.

It means

- no longer seeing women as accessories to men;
- forevermore seeing women as decision makers;

- no longer saying women ramble off the track;
- forevermore going with them to why they buy;

- no longer saying women don't know what they want;
- forevermore hearing what they value—and are prepared to pay for;

- no longer saying women can't make a decision;
- forevermore knowing their more-involved process may pay back to you many times over;

- no longer settling for the old-school try; and
- forevermore getting the new consumer math: $1 + 1 = 3$—or more.

It means from now on realizing that when you see a female customer coming your way, the thing to think about is the size of her purse. It means having your eye on the rounded shape of her wallet. It means seeing women customers for what they are: an amazing business opportunity and rich customer base.

With that, you'll be on your way to winning the toughest customer on planet Earth. From there, the sky is the limit.

(further acknowledgments)

I'd like to also acknowledge my clients who have supported me in my efforts to bring attention to the need to change how people sell and market to women. They include:

American Bankers Association
AOL
Bristol-Myers Squibb
BusinessWeek magazine
CARE Organization
Carlson Companies
Country Inns & Suites
EMI
Hewlett-Packard
Lincoln Financial
MassMutual Financial Group
Merrill Lynch
Michael Bolton

The MONY Group

Massachusetts Bankers Association

New York Bankers Association

Office Depot

PersonalShopper.com

Principal Financial

Prudential Financial

Regent Seven Seas Cruises

Sears Home Improvement

TGI Friday's

UBS Financial

UPS

Universal Records

Verizon Wireless

Washington Mutual

WM Funds

Xerox

(index)

Speaking, training, and consulting opportunities

MedeliaCommunications is a premier marketing company that supports corporations in their efforts to build market share with women and in target markets. The company provides insight and expertise in Strategic Alliances; Marketing & Sales Training; Women & Target Markets; Research Intelligence; and Entertainment Marketing.

Medelia provides extensive training in selling to women. Programs include:

- Selling to Women
- Selling to Affluent Women
- Appreciating Women in the Couple Sale
- Selling to Women Business Owners
- Selling to Target Markets
- Recruiting and Retaining Women in Sales

The new "*Winning the Toughest Customer* Training Series" includes live training, audio training and online training options.

 For more information on workbooks, audio or online training, or to book Delia Passi for sales training or speaking engagements, contact **info@medelia.com** or call 1-866-937-6996 toll-free.